EARTH AT RISK

Building a Resistance

Movement to Save

the Planet

EARTH AT RISK

Building a Resistance

Movement to Save

the Planet

Edited by Derrick Jensen and Lierre Keith

FLASHPOINT PRESS
CRESCENT CITY, CALIFORNIA

Earth at Risk: Building a Resistance Movement to Save the Planet
Edited by Derrick Jensen and Lierre Keith
© 2013 Derrick Jensen and Lierre Keith

ISBN: 978-1-60486-674-2
LCCN: 2012913623

10 9 8 7 6 5 4 3 2 1

Flashpoint Press
PO Box 903
Crescent City, CA 95531
www.flashpoint.com

PM Press
PO Box 23912
Oakland, CA 94623
www.pmpress.org

Layout by Jonathan Rowland
Cover art by Stephanie McMillan

Printed on recycled paper by the Employee Owners
of Thomson-Shore in Dexter, Michigan.
www.thomsonshore.com

Contents

Introduction by
Derrick Jensen

"This collection of discussions is about the shift in strategy and tactics that has to happen if we want to build an effective resistance. It is about putting our bodies and our lives between the industrial system and life on the planet. It is about fighting back."

The dominant culture is killing the planet. It is long past time that those of us who care about life on earth begin to take the actions necessary to stop civilization from destroying every living being.

By now we all know the statistics and trends: 90 percent of the large fish in the oceans are gone, 97 percent of native forests have been destroyed, as have 98 percent of native grasslands. There is ten times as much plastic as phytoplankton in the oceans. Amphibian populations are collapsing, migratory songbird populations are collapsing, mollusk populations are collapsing, fish populations are collapsing, and so on. Have you noticed that you don't have to clean your windshield nearly as often as you used to? Even insect populations are collapsing. Two hundred species are driven extinct each and every day.

This culture destroys landbases. That's what it *does*. Iraq used to have cedar forests so thick that sunlight never touched the ground. One of the first written myths of this culture is about Gilgamesh deforesting the hills and valleys of Iraq to build a great city. The Arabian Peninsula used to be oak savannah. The Near East was heavily forested. We've all heard of the cedars of Lebanon. Greece was heavily forested. North Africa was heavily forested. This culture destroys landbases, and it won't stop doing so because we ask nicely. We don't live in a democracy. Think about it: do governments better serve corporations or living beings? Do judicial systems hold CEOs accountable for their destructive, often murderous acts?

Here are a couple of riddles that aren't very funny. Question: What do you get when you cross a long drug habit, a quick temper, and a gun? Answer: Two life terms for murder, earliest release date 2026. Question: What do you get when you cross two nation states, a large corporation, forty tons of poison, and at least eight thousand dead human beings? Answer: Retirement with full pay and benefits. That's what happened to Warren Anderson, CEO of Union Carbide, which caused the mass murder at Bhopal.

Here's another way to say this: What do you call someone who conspires to put poison in the subways of Tokyo? You call him a terrorist and you put him in prison for life. What do you call someone who conspires to put poison in the groundwater of the United States? You call him Dick Cheney. Or oil and gas man, or fracker. Do the rich face the same judicial system as you or I? Does life on earth have as much standing in a court as does a corporation? We all know the answers to those questions. And we know in our bones, if not always our heads, that this culture won't undergo any sort of voluntary transformation to a sane and sustainable way of living.

If you care about life on the planet and if you believe the culture won't voluntarily cease to destroy it, how does that belief affect your methods of resistance? Most of us don't know because most of us don't talk about it.

At the Earth at Risk conferences of 2011 and 2012, leading environmental activists and thinkers gathered to talk about it. This collection of discussions from those days is about the shift in strategy and tactics that has to happen if we want to build an effective resistance. It is about putting our bodies and our lives between the industrial system and life on the planet. It is about fighting back.

Those who inherit whatever is left of the world once this culture has been stopped, whether through peak oil, economic collapse, ecological collapse, or the efforts of brave women and men resisting in alliance with the natural world, are going to judge us by the health of the landbase, by what we leave behind. They're not going to care how you or I lived our lives, how hard we tried, or whether we were nice people. They're not going to care whether we were violent or nonviolent. They're not going to care whether we grieve the murder of the planet. They're not going to care whether we were enlightened or not enlightened.

They're not going to care what sort of excuses we had to not act. *I'm too stressed to think about it. It's too big and scary. I'm too busy. Those in power will kill me if I act against them. If I fight back, I run the risk of becoming like they are. But I recycled.* You can substitute any of a thousand other excuses we've all heard too many times.

Those who come after us are not going to care how simply we lived. They're not going to care how pure we were in thought or action. They're not going to care whether we voted Democrat, Republican, Green, Libertarian, or not at all. They're not going to care if we wrote really big books. They're not going to care whether we had compassion for the CEOs and politicians running the deathly economy. They're going to care whether they can breathe the air and drink the water.

Every new study reveals that global warming is happening far more quickly than was previously anticipated. Scientists are now suggesting the real possibility of billions of human beings being killed off by what some are calling a "climate Holocaust." A recently released study suggests an increase in temperature of 16 degrees Celsius, or about 30 degrees Fahrenheit, by the year 2100. We're not talking about this culture killing the planet sometime in the far distant future. This is the future that children born today will see and suffer in their lifetimes. Is this culture worth more than the lives of your own children?

In *The Nazi Doctors*, Robert Jay Lifton explored how it was that men who had taken the Hippocratic oath could lend their skills to prisons where inmates were worked to death or killed in assembly lines. He found that many of the doctors honestly cared for their

charges and did everything within their power, which meant pa-
thetically little, to make life better for the inmates. If an inmate got
sick, they might give the inmate an aspirin to lick. They might put
the inmate to bed for a day or two, but not for too long, or the inmate might be selected for murder. They might kill patients with
contagious diseases to keep the diseases from spreading. All this
made sense within the confines of Auschwitz. The doctors did everything they could to help the inmates, except for the most important thing of all: they never questioned the existence of Auschwitz
itself. They never questioned working the inmates to death. They
never questioned starving them to death. They never questioned imprisoning them. They never questioned torturing them. They never
questioned poisoning them. They never questioned the existence of
a culture that would lead to those atrocities. They never questioned
the logic that leads inevitably to the electrified fences, the gas cham-
bers, the bullets in the brain.

We as environmentalists do the same. We fight as hard as we can
to protect the places we love using the tools of the system the best
we can. Yet we don't do the most important thing of all: we don't
question the existence of the whole death culture. We don't question
the existence of an economic and social system that is working the
world to death, starving it to death, imprisoning it, torturing it. We
never question the logic that leads inevitably to clearcuts, murdered
oceans, loss of topsoil, dammed rivers, and poisoned aquifers. And
we certainly don't stop these horrors.

What do all the mainstream so-called solutions to global warming have in common? They take industrial capitalism as a given, and
they operate on the assumption that the natural world must conform to industrial capitalism. That's literally insane in terms of being out of touch with physical reality, because without physical reality—without a real world—you don't have any economic system
whatsoever. Any solution to global warming, any solution to any of
these problems, has to take the real, physical world as a given, and

understand that it is the social system that must conform to the real world.

I once asked an intelligent seven-year-old, "So what will it take to stop global warming, caused in great measure by the burning of oil and gas?" the seven-year-old answered, "Stop burning oil and gas!" And I said, "You are smarter than any environmentalist I've ever met." If you ask any reasonably intelligent thirty-five-year-old who works for a green, high-tech consulting corporation, you're going to receive an answer that actually helps the corporation more than the real physical world.

When most people in this culture ask, "How can we stop global warming?" they aren't really asking what they pretend they're asking. They're asking instead, "How can we stop global warming without stopping the burning of oil and gas, without stopping the industrial infrastructure, without stopping the whole omnicidal system?" You can't. Or when people ask, "How can we save the salmon?" The answer is actually pretty straightforward: remove dams, stop industrial logging, stop industrial fishing, stop the murder of the oceans, stop global warming. But of course, what they're really asking is, "How can we save salmon without removing dams, without stopping industrial logging, without stopping industrial fishing, without stopping the murder of the oceans, without stopping global warming?" The answer: you can't.

Here's another way to look at this. What would we do if space aliens had invaded this planet and they were vacuuming the oceans and cutting down native forests and putting dams on every river and changing the climate and putting dioxin and dozens of other carcinogens into every mother's breastmilk and into the flesh of your children, lover, mother, father, brother, sister, friends, and into your own flesh? If space aliens were doing all this, would you resist? If there existed a resistance movement, would you join it? If not, why not? How much worse would the damage have to get before you stopped those killing the planet, killing those you love, killing you?

Ninety percent of the large fish in the oceans are already gone. What is your threshold for resistance? Ninety-one percent? Ninety-two? Ninety-three? Ninety-four? Would you wait until they killed off ninety-five percent? Ninety-six? Ninety-seven? Ninety-eight? Ninety-nine percent? How about one hundred percent? Would you fight back then?

* * *

People routinely approach me to tell me how their hope and despair have merged into one. Many have done everything they can to protect the places they love—everything, that is, except the most important thing of all: to bring down the culture itself. Now they want to go on the offensive. They want to stop this culture in its tracks, but they don't know how. The voices in this book take a step toward creating a culture of resistance, toward creating the conditions for salmon to be able to return, for songbirds to be able to return, for amphibians to be able to return.

Fighting back means first and foremost thinking and feeling for ourselves, finding who and what we love, and figuring out how best to defend our beloved, using the means that are appropriate and necessary. We must deprive the rich of their ability to steal from the poor and the powerful of their ability to destroy the planet. We must defend and rebuild just and sustainable human communities nestled inside repaired and restored landbases. This is a vast undertaking, but it can be done. Industrial civilization can be stopped.

We need to take direct actions against strategic infrastructure, and we need to build direct democracies based on human and nonhuman rights and sustainable material cultures. The different branches of resistance movements must work in tandem—the aboveground and belowground, the militants and the nonviolent, the frontline activists and the cultural workers. We need it all.

Finally, we need courage. The word *courage* comes from the same root as *coeur*, the French word for "heart." We need all the courage of which the human heart is capable, forged into both weapon and shield to defend what is left of this planet.

The lifeblood of courage is, of course, love. So while these discussions from the Earth at Risk conferences are about fighting back, in the end they are really about love. The songbirds and the salmon need our love because they are disappearing, slipping into that longest night of extinction. It is up to us to build a resistance from whatever comes to hand: whispers and prayers, history and dreams, and our bravest words and actions. It will often seem impossible, but we'll have to do it anyway. With love as our first cause, how can we fail?

William Catton Jr.

"Can we change humanity's aspirations to make them less habitat-destructive, without ourselves becoming misanthropic in the process? We need a sense of modesty."

Derrick Jensen: William R. Catton has written one of the twentieth century's most important books: *Overshoot: The Ecological Basis of Revolutionary Change*. William, do present economic troubles have important ecological implications that earlier hard times perhaps would not have had?

William Catton Jr.: I think that the problem with the economic view of the recession is epitomized by a statement by Senator Ron Johnson of Wisconsin. He said that we are committing "intergenerational larceny." That's a good term: intergenerational larceny. We're stealing from future generations. Unfortunately, he was thinking simply in monetary terms, saying, "We've got to get the deficit down," and so on. If people would start thinking in terms of an ecological deficit, instead of just a monetary deficit, we'd be a lot closer to understanding what our real predicament is. We are committing intergenerational larceny in terms of what we're doing to the planet.

Take, for example, the Deepwater oil disaster in the Gulf of Mexico. Most people did not really focus on the real problem there, which is that this resource that we say that we "need" is becoming so elusive that we have to go a whole mile down under the water, then drill another mile into the ground underneath that water, in order to access it. That has consequences. People in the oil industry have always been aware of oil gushers. When you strike a gusher, the pressure of the gas in the ground pushes the oil out. We should have expected that drilling underwater would be no different. We should have predicted that we'd have a gusher there in the Gulf of Mexico.

What we've got to learn from this is that the human species really has no right to punch holes in the bottom of the ocean. Oil "production" is a bad term. It should be "extraction." Humans didn't produce oil. Nature produced it. Millions of years ago, it was deposited safely underground where we couldn't reach it. Well, now we learned how to reach it, and that's why we're in trouble.

It is a fact of life that every organism and population must use the environment in three ways. Any organism has to use the environment as a source of sustenance, as a space in which it does its various activities, and as a disposal site, because we all produce something, in the process of living, that we want to get rid of. Now, in an overloaded world, this becomes a sad fact—sad as in S-A-D, which stands for Source, Activity, Disposal. I'm glad I was born in an English-speaking country, because that acronym doesn't work in other languages. Why is the fact that we all use the environment in three ways a sad fact in an overloaded world? Because it's impossible any longer to segregate each of those uses from the other two. We're in trouble because the three different uses increasingly interfere with each other.

Derrick: This question seems embarrassing, really, but given public discourse, I think it needs to be asked. Does a finite earth necessarily have ecological limits? What would you say are the most essential ecological ideas people need to know in order to understand present or future circumstances?

William: A finite earth necessarily does have ecological limits. People should open their minds and think, how is it that we can expect to go on increasing our numbers on a finite planet forever? If we are not worried at all about overdoing whatever we do, this implies that we think that it could go on forever.

For any kind of use of any particular environment, by any species, there is a rate or amount of such use that can be exceeded only by reducing the subsequent suitability of that environment for that use. If you stay below that level, then use can go on and on and on and on. But, if you exceed that level, you begin to destroy that habitat upon which you are dependent. This is true for all species. There can be too many of any particular species but, ecologically speaking, the interactions between the different species have tended to keep each other in some kind of balance. That is, until, *Homo sapiens* came along and learned ways of evading those natural restraints.

We need a good definition of carrying capacity. I began by defining it as simply the maximum sustainable load, but let's get a little more explicit. For ranchers and range managers, carrying capacity has been a familiar term for several generations. It is the maximum population of a given species that a particular environment can support indefinitely. You can exceed carrying capacity temporarily, but not permanently. What does "indefinitely" refer to there? It means the maximum load that can be supported without habitat damage. If you exceed the carrying capacity, you begin damaging the habitat.

Now, we humans are a very special species. We're special in the sense that we're the only species that could get together like this and talk, and by exchanging facts and insights achieve knowledge collectively that we might never discover individually. We're the only species that has extensive technology outside our own bodies. Darwin was fascinated by the fact that the different species of birds on the different Galapagos Islands had different shaped beaks for using different resources on the different islands. Well, their "technology" was part of their bodies. Humans have exosomatic technology, so it's as if humans are not just one species, but many species, depending on their equipment and how they are organized to use it. So, in the case of humans, carrying capacity is the maximum human population, equipped with a given assortment of technology and a given pattern of organization, that a particular environment can support indefinitely, without habitat damage. Since human habits vary among different human societies, a given environment will have different carrying capacities for different populations.

The earliest human beings gathered naturally available (and mainly renewable) sustenance materials. They were hunters and gatherers. There were very few of them, compared to the present human population of the planet. They were foragers, like all previous animal species had been.

About ten thousand years ago, humans underwent a big change by inventing processes that we call agriculture. The advent of farming meant that humans had a different relationship to the ecosystem than they'd ever had before. They began managing ecosystems to ensure that more of what they wanted would be produced, and that meant the areas they used would be producing less of some of the things that other species would be foraging for. They could sustainably have available the things that they needed because they were managing the system.

In order to do this, humans used energy from sources other than their own muscles. They used the muscles of other animals that they domesticated. They used wind power and moving water as sources of energy. But a little over two hundred years ago, they made another breakthrough: they began to use fossil fuels to provide additional amounts of energy. They became "*Homo colossus*," not just *Homo sapiens*. It was a disaster, and that's finally becoming clear.

The very fact that humans defined carbon-rich underground material as *fuel*—because it could burn and could release energy— was, in retrospect, our blunder. It was nature's sequestration of formerly atmospheric carbon, but we saw it as fuel for the taking. What we need to realize now—and people just have not recognized this fact—is that using oil this way caused us to revert to being foragers. We had made a great step forward by advancing from foraging to farming, but now we've taken a tremendous leap backward in "advancing" to foraging again. We're hell-bent on depleting exhaustible supplies of substances that we have come to desperately depend upon.

These supplies are impossible to reproduce, since they were created and put in place not by human effort, but by ancient nature. Petroleum is not renewable on any kind of human scale. Even renewable resources, such as food, are used faster than their rate of renewal.

The Irish potato famine is an example of what happens when natural renewal processes are undermined. In 1739, a big freeze killed a lot of the potato crop in Ireland, and many Irish people starved, causing the population to dip. Over the next several years Ireland had successful potato crops, and the population increased rapidly from about two million people to well over eight million. That was too many people for a land mass of Ireland's size. The population had also become dependent upon the potato as a mainstay of their sustenance. So when a fungus invaded the island and began destroying the potato crop, the population dropped sharply back down. Happily, in those days there was still surplus carrying capacity elsewhere on the planet, so many Irish people moved to North America, but there were a couple million people who met premature deaths from starvation and diseases.

Derrick: On a finite planet, why did the expectation of continuing growth and perpetual progress seem so plausible to so many people? What has changed in our time to erode the conviction that perpetual growth is possible and desirable?

William: I think we got the impression that perpetual growth was possible simply because early on there really was a carrying capacity surplus for the kind of total use of the environment of which human beings were capable. This false impression was aggravated when Europeans discovered that there was a whole second hemisphere. These two continents in the Western world seemed so enticing. They were sparsely populated, in comparison to Europe. The Indians who were here didn't count, of course, because they weren't Europeans. The notion of limitlessness was further reinforced with the slightly later European discovery of Australia, New Zealand, the Pacific Islands, and so on.

Of course, you can't go on discovering second hemispheres very long. Today, the population density of the second hemisphere is greater than the population density of the first hemisphere was at the time of the discovery. Moreover, we have become, with all of this technological equipment that we've invented in the last couple hundred years, a much larger species than we used to be. We're more numerous and also much larger in per capita resource appetite. We've made ourselves dependent upon nonrenewable resources with a vengeance, and we've become particularly dependent on vast quantities of nonrenewable energy resources. That's why the plausibility of perpetual progress has ceased.

The current recession will have an outcome different from previous recessions, because we no longer have our carrying capacity surplus. A recession in a time when you're facing a carrying capacity deficit is bound to have a different outcome from one that occurred when we could still plausibly think of stimulating renewed access to a carrying capacity surplus.

Paul Krugman, in his column for the *New York Times*, has deplored the fact that we didn't spend enough on the stimulus program. He believes Obama has made the same mistake that he thinks FDR made after the end of his first term, when people urged him to slow deficit spending. Krugman suggests that Obama is facing a predicament similar to the one FDR faced, but we're not in 1937 or 1938 anymore. There has been a hell of a lot of oil pumped out of the ground since then. We're on the downslope, and we're not discovering new deposits anywhere near as quickly as we're exhausting old deposits. Obama doesn't face the opportunities for stimulating the economy that FDR faced.

Derrick: Will ecological limits differently affect people in different parts of the world?

William: Different parts of the world will be affected differently by the ecological deficit that the world now confronts, because different parts of the world are using their local part of the world differently.

The terminology that we've invented to refer to these different parts of the world has not really been adequate. When I studied history as a kid, first in grade school and then in high school, we talked about the advanced countries and the backward countries. Later, we more or less outgrew that ethnocentric language, and we started talking about developed and underdeveloped countries. Then, we decided that even "underdeveloped" was a stigmatizing word and was not quite proper, so we started talking about developed and developing countries.

The real dichotomy is between countries that are mainly populated by *Homo colossus*—the technologically advanced, fossil fuel–ravenous, nonrenewable resource–ravenous countries—contrasted with the countries that haven't yet committed themselves so fully to depending upon exhaustible resources. That's the real difference.

The customary assumption that we tend to make on our side of the development line is that we are going to survive the coming problems better than the people on the wrong side of the line. That may be exactly the reverse of the truth. It may very well be countries that have not yet committed themselves to a ravenous use of non-renewable resources that end up better off in the long run.

Derrick: Is there a way out of all of this?

William: I hope so. This may be a little bit fanciful, but I'd like to share my favorite sentence in the English language. It is on the bronze plaques commemorating the first director of the National Park Service, Stephen Tyng Mather. The Park Service was founded in

1916, and there's a plaque to honor him in every one of our National Parks. There's a sentence at the bottom that says, "He laid the foundation of the National Park Service, defining and establishing the policies under which its areas shall be developed and conserved unimpaired for future generations." That's the key idea: the land should be conserved unimpaired for future generations. That comes awfully close to recognition of the carrying capacity concept.

That's not my favorite sentence, though. This is my favorite sentence: "There will never come an end to the good he has done." I hope that's true. What a fantastic sentence that is. Recently, I've begun wondering if there will ever come an end to the harm that some people have done.

I'm not saying that we could make the whole world a National Park, but we need to approach our usage of the planet in somewhat the same mood as Mather approached the National Parks. He wanted to preserve them unimpaired for future generations. I hope that my great-grandsons—two of whom I already know—are going to have a world that they can still enjoy, but it's not going to be the same world in which I was a little kid.

Derrick: Is it possible that humanity's future has been irreparably damaged?

William: Perhaps the answer is yes. But this conference is about trying to mount a real protest movement to bring to a halt the devastation that we've laid on this planet. To do this, we've got to remember what a multidimensional onslaught it has been. There are three issues to tackle, and choosing just one of them isn't going to do the job.

The first is that, somehow, we have to end population growth, because there are already too many of us, even if we weren't using earth with such per capita extravagance. Second, we have to stop the technological enlargement of our appetite for oil and other finite supplies. Third, we have to recognize the fact that our impact is global, not local. When I drive my car and emit CO_2 into the atmosphere, or when I breathe and emit a little bit of CO_2 into the atmosphere, it isn't just the atmosphere over and around me that is going to change in such a way that it retains more solar heat. The atmosphere over the whole world is hurt by such leaks and emissions. We're no longer just local beings. Our activities affect a wider world, not just our immediate vicinity.

These are the three prongs of the problem that has diminished our independence. Even though we are impelled to give priority to our own individual needs, we can no longer get away with doing that. Life is not that simple anymore.

I worry that we may, in our quest to devise a way of stopping all three of these development processes, become misanthropes, anti-human. Several centuries ago, the English clergyman John Donne said, "No man is an island. Every man is a piece of a continent." (Please remember that in those days "men" meant all humans, both genders.) Can we change humanity's aspirations to make them less habitat-destructive, without ourselves becoming misanthropic in the process? We need a sense of modesty.

Let me conclude with a National Parks motto. When you enter a National Park, you're admonished to enjoy and photograph the scenery, but you are not to remove or damage the actual park features, the rocks, plants, and wildlife.

Take only pictures. Leave only footprints.

Somehow, we need an equivalent guideline for our whole approach to life on this planet.

Jane Caputi

"It is deeply telling that the concept of *dirt* has become the term that means unacceptable, sinful, and horrific. This, again, is based in a mind-body split and foundational denial of the fact that humans are part of nature, part of the earth."

Derrick Jensen: Jane Caputi, better than anyone, lays out the mythological underpinnings of the destructive behavior that is killing our planet. Her book *The Age of Sex Crime* is a stunning exploration of the ways that women's bodies are cut up by patriarchy. It makes connections between the mutilation of the genitals and breasts of women by serial sex killers, unnecessary hysterectomies and breast surgeries, and how women's body parts are cut up and used for advertising. All of these manifest patriarchal imperatives to cut up the bodies of women.

Jane Caputi: Yes, and in a patriarchal culture like our own, women have become not only the "other" but simultaneously a symbolic sex. What is acted out on the female body parallels larger practices of domination, fragmentation, and conquest against the earth body, which is being polluted, strip-mined, deforested, and cut up into parcels of private property. Equally, this pattern points to the fragmentation of the psyche, which ultimately underlies and enables all of this damage.

The initial splitting of the psyche proceeds from a disavowal of interconnection and interdependency. An individual or group perceives itself as split off from creation. They deny and even demonize aspects of being (such as emotionality, carnality, mortality, need) and project these onto another individual or group. That group becomes a scapegoated "other." The "other" is said to be inferior, not a significant being with intelligence, agency, purpose, soul.

This is the framework that alleges superiority of culture over nature, civilization over savagery, mind over body, men over women, whites over blacks, and so on. Invariably, the oppressed group is the one who is identified with wild, uncontrollable, and supposedly "filthy" nature. At the same time, the one who is in control, even if female, is identified as "the man," and is identified with culture or civilization. The "man" occupies the masculine position ("on top"), while the dominated one (even if male) is identified with and put into the feminine position, becoming the underling—the "bitch," the "wimp," the "trash," and so on.

In Western culture, this process of "othering" makes the earth and women and those men identified with women into objects, "natural resources" to be exploited with impunity, not beings with purpose, will, and spirit. Supposedly, objects can be fetishized, modified, manipulated, sold, used, stolen, and even eliminated without affecting anything else. But this is folly. All of life is a whole, a continuum, and everything affects everything else—sometimes subtly, sometimes overtly. The Buddhist teacher Thich Nhat Hanh speaks to this with the concept of *interbeing*. Nobel Prize winner and founder of the Green Belt Movement Wangari Maathai refers to this same principle when she lists her first spiritual instruction for the healing of earth as the demonstration of love for the environment through our lifestyles.

We are conditioned to see the world in fragments, but we should be seeing a whole or integrated system of being, a sacred hoop connecting all, as Native science or philosophy understands it. Privileged folks in particular need to be seeing, for example, the exploitation of workers who make our "smartphones" or harvest our food, the toxic waste left by the use of fossil fuels and nuclear materials in making the electricity we take for granted, the devastated soils and pesticide contamination and ensuing illness, particularly for workers, left in the wake of agribusiness. We need to join those who have been most affected by toxic contaminations. We need to love the environment, which includes people. We need to change our lifestyles in ways that produce love, health, and justice.

Val Plumwood is a key thinker on the denial of interdependency. While oppressors proclaim their superiority and separateness, and claim that everyone else is dependent on them, the reverse is actually true. Those at the top are completely dependent on those they have forced to the bottom, those who perform "menial" labor, who clear away their trash, who feed them, who wait on them.

Oppressors identify everyone (human and nonhuman) who provides these kinds of necessary services as being closer to "nature," because of course, "nature" too provides for those on top—supposedly for free, without complaint, and without limit. One of the most fallacious conclusions of the fragmented consciousness is that "nature" is somehow separate from those on top. Polluters (dumping toxic ideologies as well as substances) wrongly believe that they can poison or exploit "lower" humans, the land, the elements, animals, and so on without ultimately poisoning themselves. This is absolute folly.

To return to the figure of the serial killer, the most iconic is Jack the Ripper. He slit the throats of his prostitute victims and then mutilated their breasts and vulvae, stealing the womb from one and fully dismembering the body of another. He didn't rape anyone, but his attacks with the knife, understood as a "phallic" weapon, were perceived as sexual acts—and, in a patriarchal, pornographic culture in which sex and violence are fused, they were.

Acts of sexualized misogyny, control, and destruction proceed from that valorized separation of "men" from nature. This alienation leads to envy and hatred mingled with desire for the life Source/Force, symbolized generally by women and women's sexual and reproductive powers. Murders resulting from this alienation are ritualistic—blood sacrifices. Sacrifice always has an intended energetic component. For example, when the patriarchal and militarist religious rulers of the Aztec Empire sacrificed women, they sought to capture the creative energy traditionally associated with the earth's fertility and then redirect this energy into fueling the needs and purposes of the Empire, turning "sex" (fecundity, creativity, ecstasy) into violence. The serial sex killer, too, is a kind of patriarchal priest who sacrifices women to seize elemental energy.

The link between the serial killer and mainstream patriarchal institutions is examined in the 1963 film *Dr. Strangelove*, in which the military madman who sets off world nuclear destruction, the ultimate mutilation of the earth womb, is aptly named General Jack D. Ripper. For both the real Jack the Ripper and his filmic namesake, the attack, ultimately, is against the earth, the matrix in which life develops. This original and enduring source is the force that has been spoken of throughout human awareness, past and present, as Mother Nature.

Derrick: What is the meaning and value of the terms "Mother Nature" and "Mother Earth"?

Jane: A lot of people resist using these terms, because patriarchal culture has so distorted the practice and conceptual basis of motherhood. Mothering is supposed to be something only women do, a biological condition. Mothers are supposed to be innately self-sacrificing, unconditionally loving, and willing to clean up any mess you make. They also are supposed to prefer sons to daughters and to remain socially, economically, and intellectually powerless. Some distorted understandings of Mother Earth or Nature are based in that horrific framework.

The true essence of Mother Earth predates these misconceptions. There are many linguistic associations with nature as a mothering power. The word *nature* itself comes from a Latin root that means "to be born." The word *matter* comes from the same root as *mother*. Religious studies scholar Catherine Roach tells us that that the concept of Mother Earth or Mother Nature is probably the

oldest human religious concept. That mothering power is not equated solely with women or with biological human motherhood, but is
more properly understood as a principle that manifests in a variety
of ways, through creation and procreation as well as natural decay
and death. Mother Earth is sexual and intelligent, and her power
is fructifying, sustaining, and diverse. It is the life and death force,
in which everyone—female, male, asexual, polysexual, intersexual,
transgendered—all necessarily participate. Stepping outside of the
sexist framework, we see that the Mother is more accurately understood as Mother, Lover, Other, the source of life, transformation,
and enduring Mystery.

The dominant patriarchal culture worships the sole (if absent)
parent known as the Supreme Father God, and Mother Nature
is backgrounded, trivialized, and even demonized. There is a long
mythic tradition where patriarchal gods conquer the goddess representing the originating matrix or source, as in the stories of Tiamat,
Coyolxauhqui, and Medusa. The earth-based goddess is then replaced by the Father God, who is immaterial, purely spirit, sexless,
and lives in some abstract place called "Heaven." This patriarchal
belief that "God" lives apart from earth is one that, as Linda Hogan
avers in *Dwellings*, "has taken us toward collective destruction. It is
a belief narrow enough to forget the value of matter, the very thing
that soul inhabits."

Again, this is what we need to remember: there is not, nor can
there be, any real separation between humans and nature. When
speaking of Mother Nature we honor the wisdom of our ancestors.
Try to forget all those mocking images of nagging, shrewish, irra-
tional, and silly women, and consider "Her" as the power that fos-
ters material reality, the force that binds matter and spirit, that fires
the ongoing process of life. That process involves continuous birth,
growth, sustenance, wasting, aging, death, decay, transformation, and
rebirth, which together take shape in a great round. Understanding
the integrity and interconnectedness of this principle means living

in a participatory and reciprocal way with nonhuman nature, not only taking but giving, and most especially not putting humans as somehow above or outside of that circle.

Derrick: What is the relationship between violence against women, gay people, Native Americans, blacks, and other stigmatized groups, and violence against nonhuman nature?

Jane: In *The Rape of the Wild*, Andrée Collard warns that what happens to people, land, and animals is ultimately the same thing. Violent acts tend to be committed first upon those people who are maligned as supposedly more "natural," more "animalistic," more ruled by their sex organs, less intelligent, less rational, more "dirty." Ruling men and their female collaborators justify domination by claiming that they represent civilization and that everyone else is less evolved. Many nineteenth-century American soap ads represent Native Americans as "savages" who are inherently dirtier than white Americans. Nazis used the same paradigm to exalt Aryans and stigmatize Jews, "Gypsies," and disabled people. Homophobic discourses invariably represent lesbians and gay men as filthy and polluting. A couple of years ago an international gay pride parade was scheduled in Jerusalem and Islamic, Jewish, and Christian leaders (all men, of course) put aside their differences to try to stop the parade.

There is an ad for Diesel jeans that shows a dark-skinned woman laid out prone on zebra-patterned sheets. Her jeans are unzipped to signify that she is open, available for rape or for colonization. The small print says, "Right now, there are far too many dangerous animals running around, wasting space, wasting time, using the planet as a toilet! Take our advice. Don't be fooled by 'natural' beauty, stick 'em in practical, easy-to-clean metal cages." I'm sure the makers of this ad would defend themselves by saying that it is supposed to be a joke. But if there were anything satirical about it, they would have used a white man in a business suit. By associating this woman with filth and waste, the ad uses language and imagery that historically has justified genocide, or what is euphemistically called "ethnic cleansing." Colonizers, militaries, corporations, and governments have long been engaged in caging the land and "purifying" (that is, destroying) its inhabitants, including humans and nonhumans.

This ideology of purity is inherently not only a genocidal and homophobic one, but also a gynocidal and geocidal one. Historically it has been used to split women into "virgin" and "whore" categories, with the "virgins" being kept under house arrest, and the "whores" consigned to the street, where they can be raped, assaulted, and killed with impunity. The same rhetoric has been used to justify humans extirpating species—under the guise of "cleaning" the land of so-called "varmints," "pests," or "weeds." It is deeply telling that the concept of *dirt* has become the term that means unacceptable, sinful, and horrific. This, again, is based in a mind-body split and foundational denial of the fact that humans are part of nature, part of the earth.

Human comes from the Latin word *humus*, meaning dirt, earth. Once the patriarchal god is understood as removed from the earth, the earth and the earthy, including carnality and sexuality, becomes suspect, inferior. This erotophobia drives the destruction of all that is defined as wild "nature." Erotophobes historically have defined nature as a "virgin" for men to possess, or a dangerous witch or whore to chasten and control. Elias Farajajé-Jones observes that European colonizers perceived Indigenous people as sexually perverse due to their egalitarian, diverse, and tolerant sex and gender practices, and as evil because they found divinity in the given world, rather than a church. While colonizers were enslaving Africans and committing genocide against the peoples and lands of the Americas, those back at home in Europe were assiduously linking women to sex, nature, and evil, creating an ideology of demonic witchcraft. This led to the torture and murder of countless women, girls, and some boys and men as "witches" over three centuries. Not surprisingly, all of these atrocities were and are committed in the name of God.

Even supposedly environmentally friendly modern-day ads, promoting organic mattresses, air filters, foods, and so on, often show perfect-looking white people in pristine environments. These participate, too, in ecocidal and erotophobic discourse by promoting this suspect idea of "purity." We must never forget that we are all dirt, made from earth, and we are all equally earthy—that is, alive.

Derrick: What kinds of popular images teach us to worship domination and disrespect of the earth?

Jane: I speak of the "pornography of everyday life." When I use the word "pornography" to mean something problematic, this does not mean that I am opposed to sex and sexual stories and pictures. I fully support erotic practices and representations. I use "pornography" to designate a patriarchal habit of ideas, actions, and representations based in sexualized violence, denigration, domination, voyeurism, and objectification. This is precisely the kind of sexuality that is inculcated by an erotophobic system that includes both religion and the porn industry, working essentially hand in glove to define sexuality as something that keeps women in their inferior place.

Pornographic images show men dominating and degrading women (or a man or boy put in the "feminine" position) in sexually charged ways, or women conflated with or shown (however glamorously) as objects and dismembered body parts. Significantly, the earth is treated in much these same ways in popular imagery. An image published in the *San Francisco Examiner* at the end of the twentieth century illustrates an article on the approaching millennium and shows God the Father as an old white man with a beard up in the clouds, looking down on earth and reaching out a finger to touch the planet. This picture graphically illustrates not so much "God," but the patriarchal ego, which deems itself superior, literally above it all. The earth is no longer the matrix, the source, the creator of life, but rather a thing that was made and can be righteously unmade by that "God."

A parallel image from the frontispiece of a sixteenth-century manual for Spanish conquistadores shows a ship captain standing over a globe. He holds a divider in one hand, its tip touching the globe; his other hand fingers his sword's hilt. The text below the picture reads, "*With the compass and the sword/ More and more and more and more.*" In other words, the male conqueror, with his phallic instruments, can conquer and amass unlimited wealth.

This pattern of a white male figure spatially and conceptually dominating a passive earth body is reiterated throughout contemporary popular imagery. In ads for all manner of products, disproportionately huge men stand over the earth, spin earth on their fingers like toy tops, crush it in their hands, or blow it out of their mouths like a piece of bubble gum. The political cartoonist David Levine, in one 1985 work, makes explicit the undertone of rape that underlies these types of images: it shows Henry Kissinger fucking the body of a woman whose head is the planet earth.

The earth and women are often treated in similar, disrespectful ways. For example, an ad for ChaseShop.com advises viewers to "Shop the World," picturing the earth placed in a shopping bag. Compare this ad to a fashion photo that features ultrathin celebrity-icon Victoria Beckham. She has been dumped into a shopping bag, and her legs, splayed and adorned with high heels, spill out over the edges. Aimed directly into our unconscious, these images train us, subliminally, to comprehend both women and the earth as objects to consume and, ultimately, to throw away and replace with something else. Don't forget that the meanings of the verb *consume* include to waste, squander, and destroy completely. These are key images for the "Consumer Society."

Derrick: How else does patriarchal religion contribute to disrespect for, and violence against, the earth?

Jane: Well, we can start at the supposed beginning with the biblical story of the Garden of Eden and the drama of Eve's supposed sin, which included eating an apple of knowledge and speaking with a serpent. Looking at this story through a green consciousness, we realize that the serpent is representative of the Earth spirit, the Goddess even, an aspect of Eve herself whose name (*Hawa*) means "serpent." Eve's sin has been equated with having consensual sex, seeking knowledge, conversing with elemental beings, and initiating Adam. These are not sins but the practices associated with behaving in a respectful and loving relationship with the environment. But, of course, "God" condemns Eve and throws the pair out of the garden, commanding Adam to subdue and dominate the land, animals, and Eve.

This moment is seen by Christians as divine justification for male domination of everyone and everything. It provides the foundation for an abiding sense of alienation, as humans have now been forcibly separated from the great round of being.

This moment also prescribes the *dis-spiriting* of nonhuman nature. In prepatriarchal times as well as parts of the modern world where earth wisdom prevails, all of life is recognized as conscious, purposeful, ensouled. The ancient name for nature spirits who inhabit trees, streams, and other members of the earth community is *daemons*. The Catholic Church condemned these "demons" as evil and obscene, which led to a complete denial of their existence. All of nature was systematically dis-spirited, said to be soulless, "mere" matter.

Another germane patriarchal myth concerns the Sumerian Gilgamesh, the hero of civilization. In a quest to become immortal, Gilgamesh, the patriarchal ego writ large, sets out to kill the guardian of the forest, Huwawa, so that he will be able to cut down all the trees and make a name for himself. In other words, once dis-spirited, the forest becomes vulnerable to exploitation and destruction.

Derrick: The trees that Gilgamesh cut down were in Iraq, where cedar forests used to be so thick that sunlight never touched the ground. When people think of Iraq, they don't normally think of cedar forests so thick that sunlight never touched the ground.

Jane: No, we are only supposed to think of Iraq as the "Enemy."

Significantly, Europe's sacred groves were also razed. The Catholic Church deliberately cut down the trees because these groves were the places where people gathered to practice earth sacred rituals. St. Augustine, in particular, railed against the "filthy" and "obscene" forest daemons people communicated with in these rites.

In both cases, leaders of erotophobic patriarchal religions saw the nonhuman world as sexual, fecund, ecstatic, and most importantly, infuriatingly beyond their control. Christians eventually went from dismembering trees to burning witches. Many continue to eagerly anticipate the destruction of the Earth, prophesied in the Bible as the final elimination of all the elemental spirits. This is supposed to be a good thing, the day the "Lord" comes back to earth.

Mary Daly writes that patriarchy is a global religion whose essential message is necrophilia. By this, she means not so much a love of actual death, but of biophobic practices based in the desire to "defeat" death and arrest the movement of the life force, to fix beings into simulated and artificial forms. This necrophilia can take various forms: amassing stuff and surrounding oneself with objects; preferring a virtual human-made world to the given one; identifying with machines; trying to maintain perfect control over everything and everyone, including oneself; worshipping weaponry; massacring human and nonhuman others.

Gilgamesh wanted to attain immortality, another necrophilic aspiration. It takes contemporary form in the "posthumanist" goal to "free" humans from death. Posthumanists look forward to the day when people (rich ones, anyway) can download their consciousness into computers and supposedly then live forever, bodiless and purely mechanized. They wish to become just like that perfect, bodiless, heavenly god they worship, and to finally abandon Mother Nature. This is the logical outcome of a worldview whose imagery depicts men holding the earth in their hands as if they control it, as if the fate of the earth depends on them. But, of course, it is the Earth who holds us.

The necrophilic desire to destroy and replace Mother Nature shows up in the ubiquitous advertisements featuring artificial-looking women. Perhaps the most well-known image of this type is that scary figure in the Svedka vodka ads. The human model is altered to look like a pure white, mechanical, hairless, eminently unnatural, seemingly wombless and cuntless fembot. She seems to represent a future where technology has succeeded in triumphing over Mother Nature and Earth. Indeed, she is usually shown as out in space or in some virtual setting. But if you look deeply, you might intuit that this figure is really a horrifying visage signaling Nature's most fearsome face, in response to the consummate disrespect directed toward her. This is the face of a Sterility Goddess, promising not continuance but cessation.

Derrick: I've always thought that one of the reasons that the patriarchal god is so nasty is that he's lived six billion years and he doesn't have a body, which means he's never had an orgasm. He hates bodies.

Jane: Yes, his phallic "omnipotence" means that he is all-powerful in the sense of dominating everyone and everything. But, of course, we all know that potency means the ability to "get it up." *Omnipotence* really means, then, permanently potent, permanently hard, which I suppose also means that the Omnipotent never actually "comes." "The Omnipotent" (which is what the Catholic Church calls this god) can be understood, then, as not only a figment, but a phallus, an artificial and perpetually erect penis symbol or substitute. This is a great pornographic fantasy, I suppose, but it is deeply erotophobic. The phallus is an object; it cannot feel and it cannot connect.

Men and women are habituated to associate the (unreal) phallus—and hence the penis—with weapons, which leads not only to men's violence against women, but to an overall sexualization of violence. For example, an article in a men's magazine about male infertility shows a large handgun pointing at the viewer. The copy reads, "Why isn't your wife pregnant yet? You could be shooting blanks." This ruling notion of the penis as a weapon/phallus further separates men from nature and also separates the penis from the man. It denies the sensuous carnality and fleshy reality of the penis: sometimes soft, sometimes hard, fertile and life-giving. The penis, innately, is more like a flower than a weapon.

I like the word *cunctipotent* as an alternative word to *omnipotent*; it also means "all-powerful," but not in the sense of power over all, but as the power of the all. Cunctipotence is the power of the Mother/Lover/Other, who embraces all, whose embrace is all.

Derrick: Another thing that strikes me about the patriarchal god is that he's omnipotent, he's omniscient, he's the only god, and he's still jealous. I think we need some cosmic therapy.

Jane: I agree. But the kind of talk therapy we need doesn't come when we talk only to humans; we need to commune with nonhumans.

It's important to remember that the patriarchal god is not necessarily "real." There is not some cosmic force on the side of evil, or even "good" as they define it. Whenever Andrea Dworkin talks about the patriarchal god, she says "the God who does not exist." The patriarchal god, as a projection of the grandiose, but tenuous and heavily defended patriarchal ego, is imagined as separate from and dominant over everything "feminine." Of course, there is some kind of concentrated energy that issues from all those egos imagining themselves as "God." But it doesn't mean that this "God" has any substance.

I think it's really important—along with all of the other activisms that are necessarily part of our work—to engage in psychic activism. We do this in part by publicly disavowing belief in toxic ideologies, such as racism, sexism, homophobia, ableism, ageism, and so on. For many, this includes disavowing belief in that purely male and immaterial "God." In this kind of active disbelief, we deprive the oppressive system of needed energy, sustenance. In the film *The Matrix*, humans were kept in a state of ignorance so that they would never know that it was their life force that the machines needed to function. To undo the machines, people had to stop believing in the artificially constructed world and reclaim their energies for themselves, reclaiming at the same time their reality.

Susan Griffin, Mary Daly, Derrick, and I have all talked about how we need to stop perceiving with the very split "mind" that got us into this mess. The dominant culture deliberately discredits alternative perceptions of reality and alternative ways of knowledge. For example, the model of rationality that now rules scorns as unreal any practices of communicating with elemental beings—trees, other animals, and those kinds of presences traditionally understood as "elementals," the spirits who animate earth, air, water, and fire. It is very important to participate in that communication and thereby acknowledge our ongoing relation to and with all beings. That communication takes form in many ways, including through powers of dreaming. Dreaming, Greg Cajete says, is a natural way of accessing knowledge from the earth. It is very important to remember, as Mary Daly avers, that these ways of knowledge, like dreaming, intuition, and communication with elemental beings, are not "supernatural," but actually Super Natural, meaning they are powers that derive from being embodied, Earth beings.

If you have read George R.R. Martin's wonderful and spiritually abundant series, *A Song of Ice and Fire* (beginning with *A Game of Thrones*), you know that some of the characters experience that kind of dreaming, which they recognize as "green dreams," psychic ones that are rooted in the verdant world of forests, sunlight, soil, and the green origins of life. *Greenness* is a metaphysical property as well as a physical one. A green dream that I had many years ago (and before reading Martin) had a big influence on me. It began in an aboveground mass transit station, and suddenly there was a stairway that went down into another world. The nonhuman people there didn't really like humans, but they ignored us and we went on a long train ride before disembarking onto a road in verdant countryside. There, coming out of the earth was this flowing spring of internally sparkling greenness. (I later realized this was connected to Aldo Leopold's vision of "green fire.") I put my arm in the flow and felt ecstatic energy. Suddenly, the dreamscape switched, and I was in New Mexico, talking to a friend of mine in waking life—an Indian woman from one of the Pueblos on the Rio Grande. I asked her, what does it mean? She said, "Feed the Green." In other words, we must feed the Source that feeds us. We have to give back, literally. We have to nourish the earth in ways both physical and spiritual.

Derrick: A question I get a lot is, "Derrick, you say that the tree told you to write this, and you're encouraging people to listen to their dreams or to listen to trees. How do you do that?" Having not been taught to value that, how does one learn to decolonize in that way, and how have you personally learned how to listen?

Jane: Paula Gunn Allen and Alice Walker also endorse talking to trees and paying attention to your dreams, so we are in good company. Of course, we also have to be willing, above all, to *listen* to trees and other elemental beings, to try to hear, see and understand them on their own terms.

Patriarchal cultures only value activity, which they associate with the masculine. But we also have to be receptive. Just as the serpent offered the gift to Eve (who rightly accepted it), elemental communication really is all about our learning to accept the gift, to then offer that gift to others, and also to return gifts—energies, devotion, attention, care, and so on—to the Source.

We can start out by being receptive to the messages and gifts we encounter every day. Of course, frequently we are too distracted and too absorbed in the human world to notice. Lame Deer talks about how contemporary humans have to get away from all of these square screens that we're peering into all of the time, and he was saying this even before personal computers, smartphones, and iPads existed. We have to get back to the perceptions that come with roundness. We have to go outside, physically and otherwise, and *encounter* the cultures and the presences of elemental and non-human-beings, as well as the larger Mystery. When you read the biographies and the autobiographical and philosophical writings of Rachel Carson and Aldo Leopold, Gloria Anzaldúa and Alice Walker, you see over and over the transformations that occurred when they became receptive to such encounters. Margaret Atwood once said that the concept for her eco-philosophical novel *Oryx and Crake* came to her from the crakes, when she encountered a flock of them in Australia. Little birds really do tell us things. Of course, at the same time, we also have to develop powers of discernment, understanding the difference between actual communications and our fantasies. The discerning person recognizes efficacy as the key factor in this distinction. As the adage holds, "The proof of the pudding is in the eating," which basically means, look to the results.

Mary Daly suggests that we deeply remember our original, elemental memories, that we get in touch with the sense of connection to the All that we had as children. This is so akin to returning to *play*. Go outside, feel the earth directly through your toes, say hello to the creatures you encounter, send out a song, get to know the beings—flora and fauna and even the spirits, if you will—who live in the same place you do, while always respecting their lives and boundaries. Don't be afraid to get a little bit dirty.*

*With thanks to Ceti Boundy for her ideas on this.

Suggested Readings:

Abram, David. *The Spell of the Sensuous*. New York: Vintage, 1996.

Allen, Paula Gunn. "The Woman I Love Is a Planet; The Planet I Love Is a Tree." In *Reweaving the World: The Emergence of Ecofeminism*. Eds. I. Diamond and G.F. Orenstein. San Francisco: Sierra Club Books, 1990, 52–57.

Anzaldúa, Gloria. *Borderlands/La Frontera*. San Francisco: Spinsters/Aunt Lute Press, 1987.

Anzaldúa, Gloria. *Interviews/Entrevistas*. Ed. AnaLouise Keating. New York: Routledge, 2000.

Cajete, Greg. *Native Science: Natural Laws of Interdependence*. Santa Fe: Clear Light Publishers, 2000.

Caputi, Jane. *The Age of Sex Crime*. Bowling Green, Ohio: Bowling Green State University Popular Press, 1987.

Caputi, Jane. *Gossips, Gorgons, and Crones: The Fates of the Earth*. Santa Fe: Bear and Company, 1993.

Caputi, Jane. "Cunctipotence: Elemental Female Potency." *Trivia: Voices of Feminism*, 2006, http://www.triviavoices.net/.

Caputi, Jane. *The Pornography of Everyday Life*. Berkeley Media, 2007, www.berkeleymedia.com.

Caputi, Jane. "Feeding Green Fire." *Journal for the Study of Religion, Nature and Culture* 5, no. 4 (2011): 410–36.

Collard, Andree, and Joyce Contrucci. *Rape of the Wild: Man's Violence against Animals and the Earth*. Bloomington: Indiana University Press, 1988.

Daly, Mary. *Gyn/Ecology: The Metaethics of Radical Feminism*. Boston: Beacon Press, 1978.

Daly, Mary. *Pure Lust: Elemental Feminist Philosophy*. Boston: Beacon Press, 1984.

Farajajé-Jones, Elias. "Holy Fuck." In *Male Lust: Pleasure, Power, and Transformation*. Eds. Kerwin Kay, Jill Nagle, and Baruch Gould. New York: Harrington Park Press, 2000, 327–36.

Fire, John (Lame Deer), and John Erdoes. *Lame Deer: Seeker of Visions*. Lincoln: University of Nebraska Press, 2002.

Griffin, Susan. "Split Culture." In *Healing the Wounds: The Promise of Ecofeminism*. Ed. Judith Plant. Philadelphia: New Society Publishers, 1989, 7–17.

Hanh, Thich Nhat. *The Heart of Understanding*. Berkeley: Parallax Press, 1988.

Hogan, Linda. *Dwellings: A Spiritual History of the Living World*. New York: Touchstone Books, 1995.

Leopold, Aldo. *A Sand County Almanac: With Essays on Conservation from Round River*. New York: Ballantine Books, 1966.

Lorde, Audre. "Uses of the Erotic: The Erotic as Power." In *Sister Outsider*. Trumansburg, New York: The Crossing Press, 1984, 53–59.

Lytle, Mark Hamilton. *The Gentle Subversive: Rachel Carson, Silent Spring, and the Rise of the Environmental Movement*. New York: Oxford, 2007.

Maathai, Wangari. *Replenishing the Earth: Spiritual Values for Healing Ourselves and the World*. New York: Doubleday, 2010.

Margulis, Lynn, and Dorian Sagan. *What Is Life?* New York: Simon and Schuster, 1995.

Merchant, Carolyn. *The Death of Nature: Women, Ecology, and the Scientific Revolution*. San Francisco: Harper and Row, 1980.

Plumwood, Val. *Feminism and the Mastery of Nature*. New York: Routledge, 1993.

Roach, Catherine M. "Mother Nature Imagery." In *The Encyclopedia of Religion and Nature*, Ed. Bron R. Taylor. New York: Thoemmes Continuum, 1107–10.

Shiva, Vandana. *Staying Alive: Women, Ecology and Survival in India*. London: Zed Books, 1988.

Sjöö, Monica, and Barbara Mor. *The Great Cosmic Mother: Rediscovering the Religion of the Earth*. San Francisco: HarperSanFrancisco, 1991.

Smith, Andrea. *Conquest: Sexual Violence and American Indian Genocide*. Boston: South End Press, 2005

Walker, Alice. *Living by the Word: Selected Writings 1973–1987*. San Diego: Harcourt Brace Jovanovich, 1988.

White, Lynn. "The Historical Roots of Our Ecological Crisis." In *This Sacred Earth: Religion, Nature, Environment*. Ed. Roger S. Gottlieb. New York: Routledge, 1996, 184–93.

Riki Ott

"We must turn our backs on the existing power structure and do what the Abolitionists and the Suffragists did. They saw that the power to fix the problems lay within them. We, too, are going to use our power and our passion to create the world we want to live in. We are going to live by *our* ideals, and we'll do it so long, and so hard, and so passionately that we'll drag the existing power structure with us."

Riki Ott: I am part of a national grassroots campaign called Move to Amend, which I cofounded through Ultimate Civics, a project of Earth Island Institute, back in 2009. Move to Amend rapidly became a national movement after the *Citizens United* decision where the Supreme Court ruled that corporate persons are entitled to free speech—meaning unlimited spending—to influence election campaigns. Move to Amend is about abolishing corporate personhood—the illegitimate notion that corporations are entitled to the same rights as living, breathing human beings.

Most of our environmental and social woes are rooted in corporate personhood. We've developed a mindset that allows us to be colonized, to believe we have to live the way we live. I'd like to talk about changing people's minds, because people's minds have to change before the culture can be changed, and before the Constitution can be amended.

First, some background. My activism started with the *Exxon Valdez* oil spill of March 24, 1989, which I could see from my plane as I flew over the area. I was so traumatized by this sight that when we went to Valdez to refuel the plane, I thought to myself, what can one person do to fix something like this? This realization popped into my head: "I know enough to make a difference. Do I care enough?" I flashed back to my childhood to remember how I got to this place, at this time, with this knowledge, and I felt like a little chess piece on a giant board with an invisible hand moving me around. I realized that the universe gives you a choice. When everything is revealed, you have a choice: step up or step back.

My father sued the state of Wisconsin to stop the use of DDT there. He prevailed in 1971, and the rest of the nation banned DDT in 1972. My dad was my hero, but I realized on March 24, 1989, that the real lesson from that experience was that when a problem lies at your feet, you just need the courage to step up. I realized that the *Exxon Valdez* oil spill was my DDT. Today's youth have yet another DDT: climate crisis. We've gone from DDT to oil spills to climate chaos, and the place to begin solving these problems is inside ourselves. We have to reach inside and pull out our gifts and tackle what is at our feet.

When I first learned of the BP disaster of 2010, I knew what would happen. I had heard all of the lies before, I had seen the cover-up before, and, frankly, I didn't want to go through it all again. But I decided I couldn't hide, and I went down to the Gulf to see how I could help the people avoid the mistakes we made with the *Exxon Valdez* disaster—the biggest of which was believing Exxon when it said, "We will make you whole." Silly us. We still have toxic oil buried on our beaches in Prince William Sound. I used to take high school students out to the oiled beaches. We'd dig a pit about a foot and a half down. The surrounding beach rock is so porous, and so filled with oil, that the oil would actually flow into the pit and rise back up to the surface. This is still the state of our beaches. Scientists say it is probably going to be fifty more years before the oil fully degrades or breaks down. They have no idea when the ecosystem will recover. When a beach undergoes this kind of devastation, what do you think happens to all of the animals that breed on that beach, feed and forage on that beach, rear their young on that beach? I went down to the Gulf to tell people they would need a Plan B.

I also wanted to help the sick BP workers. I've been dealing with sick, disabled, and dying *Exxon Valdez* workers for twenty-one years, and I wanted to see if that could be avoided in the Gulf. I arrived in Venice, Louisiana, on May 5, 2010, to give my first talk to the Louisiana Shrimp Association, and what did I hear? I heard that fishermen out on the in-situ burning teams were sick—they were having trouble breathing, they had bad headaches, and their throats and eyes were burning. I found that the exact same federal policies with the exact same exemptions and loopholes that failed to protect workers' health and safety decades ago in Prince William Sound were still in place. Nothing had changed. BP was using outdated laws to reduce its liability for paying to take care of its workers. I'd never thought I'd say that *Exxon Valdez* was a cakewalk, but it was compared to what happened in the Gulf.

Hurricane Creekkeeper John Wathen managed to get the only footage of what I came to call the "death gyres," the rip currents that collected dead animals offshore. The Incident Command—BP and the U.S. Coast Guard—kept the media 1,500 feet up in the air so the press couldn't really capture the situation there. The animal carcasses were corralled, taken out to sea, and dumped at night, according to fishermen who were involved with so-called "Night-time Operations." Offshore workers reported "thousands of dolphins, birds too numerous to count, sea turtles too numerous to count," and even whales in the death gyres. Keep in mind that you should add two zeros—one hundred times—to these numbers. I say that based on scientific studies of carcass drift in Alaska, where only 1 percent of the carcasses were actually recovered.

History repeated itself because BP used the same mechanical cleanup technology that didn't work with *Exxon Valdez*: booms. Booms are erected to keep oil out of certain areas, but oil gets on the inside of the boom by jumping under or over it, and then the boom actually holds the oil close instead of keeping the oil away. In this way, unattended booms kept oil pinned inside of marshes and against barrier islands for hundreds of miles along the Gulf coast.

Then you have the tragedy of the civilians. In Alaska, we don't have miles of populated beaches. In the Gulf there are about four to five million people living where the oil came ashore, and millions more visitors. The dispersant came ashore in the air, in the water, and in the rain. People got sick. I took pictures on beaches where, facing in one direction, I could see HAZMAT workers with their boots taped to their pants legs to avoid getting contaminated, while in the other direction children swam in areas with dispersant and oil. The HAZMAT workers had been told by BP's safety trainers that the ocean was contaminated, and they were to stay fifteen feet away. But the public officials declared that the beach was open and the same ocean was safe to swim in.

I got a lot of phone calls from Gulf residents and visitors after they'd spent time at the beach, and they and their little children are sick now. The officials who said it was safe are downplaying that, of course. There were five federal agencies out there, and they couldn't find anything toxic in the air or the water, but I had no problem documenting a large number of common symptoms across the Gulf, from Terrebonne Parish in Louisiana on the west side of Barataria Bay, all the way over to Apalachicola, Florida, in the crook of the panhandle. I saw the exact same symptoms that occurred with *Exxon Valdez* workers: dry coughs, headaches, sore throats, dizziness, nose bleeds, ear bleeds, eye problems, peeling hands, bad skin rashes. Not only were these symptoms common among workers on the *Exxon Valdez* oil spill, they also were common among people exposed to oil after the *Prestige* spill in Spain and the *Hebei Spirit* spill in South Korea, and among residents of Fort Chipewyan in Canada, which is downstream of the Alberta Tar Sands development. The symptoms have also occurred in communities close to fracking (hydraulic fracturing) activities in the Rocky Mountain states and in Pennsylvania.

Oil is toxic to life on the planet. This is being downplayed by our federal government and by the oil companies. I can't exactly take a picture of a cough or a sore throat, but I know people who are on their fourth round of antibiotics, and their symptoms are not going away. Antibiotics are not making people better, because it's not a biological problem; it's a chemical one. The petrochemical industry rules down in Mississippi and Louisiana. The doctors do not challenge the petrochemical industry, so they do not diagnose chemical illnesses. People are being misdiagnosed and suffering in the short term, and they are not going to get better in the long term without proper treatment for chemical illnesses.

I traveled back and forth across the Gulf giving talks, encouraging people to start problem solving. If they didn't like what they were hearing, if the government's reality wasn't matching their own, what was it that they wanted to do? I kept encouraging them to come up with the answers. I asked if they thought there was a problem with the air quality. Yes, they did. "What can we do?" they asked. "What do you want to do?" I asked. Well, can we take our own air quality samples? Can we take our own water quality samples? Yes. I told them about proper sampling methods and analytical labs. So people did that—they took samples and sent the samples off to labs. This happened in the Deep South, where people have a very colonized mindset; they are very acquiescent to authority.

Before I went to the Gulf, I had a conversation with George Lakoff in Berkeley. I was excited to tell him all about Move to Amend. He said, "Great idea. What are you doing to organize in the Deep South?" I said, "Nothing." Lakoff's point was that we cannot have a national movement without the Deep South, and his point was well taken. I would like to have a do-over of that conversation now that I've made the South a focus of my activism.

As I traveled back and forth across the Gulf states after the disaster, people showed me the results of their air quality samples and their water quality samples—and the levels of toxic chemicals were very high. People told me they were sick and asked how could they prove that they were sick because of what they were finding in the air and water. I told them that to prove that, we would need to take blood samples. I talked about the connection between the air we breathe, the water we drink or swim in, the food we eat, and what shows up in our blood. If we are living, breathing, and swimming in an oiled environment, or eating oiled food, the oil will show up in our blood. People got it. They started nonprofit organizations and raised $300 for each of the sickest people to pay for blood tests to find out if the oil was in their blood. Sure enough, the tests came back showing that people were in the upper ninety-fifth percentile, nationwide, for oil in their blood. People realized the oil was flowing straight from the Gulf Stream into their bloodstreams. I'm sure the test results delighted a ton of lawyers, but they terrified residents.

What's the official story? The National Oceanic and Atmospheric Administration (NOAA), Environmental Protection Agency (EPA), and Centers for Disease Control (CDC) say that oil and dispersants are not toxic, because the same ingredients that are in dispersants are in Klondike ice cream bars, ibuprofen, household cleaning products, lip gloss, skin repair cosmetics, and more. NOAA and BP teamed up to visit eighth-grade classrooms in the Gulf to show children how to safely clean up an oil spill. They spilled cocoa powder in a little aquarium to mimic an oil spill—cocoa powder, right? Yummy. Then they sprinkled in Dawn dish soap to "disperse" the oil. "See, children? Dispersant works to clean up the oil, and we're going to save the world. It's okay."

The saddest and scariest part of the BP disaster for me was the realization that our federal administration—the Obama adminis-tration, Mr. Hope—has no exit strategy to get America off oil or coal. It really is all up to us. In the Gulf, it didn't take people twenty years like with the *Exxon Valdez* spill to realize the federal govern-ment was not in control of the situation; it took them two months. By mid-June after the April spill, people in the Gulf started to ask me, "What's happening? Isn't this America? Why is BP in charge?" I told them that our democracy has been hijacked by large corpora-tions. I said this to fundamental Christians to the right of right, con-servatives, tea party people, and oilmen. People from audience after audience came up after my talks to let me know that I had not said anything that offended them. I was asked to come back to the Gulf to give democracy trainings. They told me they didn't care about

BP's money, but they cared about their culture. They wanted their community back. Always, they asked, "What can we do?" I kind of live for the "What can we do?" question.

We were given a structure of government with three branches. If one of the branches runs amok, there is a system of checks and balances to rebalance power. But if one branch *really* runs amok, it's up to We the People to fix it. We are the ultimate check.

Our U.S. Supreme Court ran amok back in 1886, when it allowed corporations to have constitutional rights, which became known as corporate personhood. Humans are born with inalienable rights—rights that cannot be transferred or surrendered to nonhuman entities. In 1886, the Supreme Court decided that corporations were entitled to be treated equal to humans, and that this meant giving them constitutional protections, rights. From that erroneous and illegitimate decision, a body of law grew that became known as the doctrine of corporate constitutional rights. This facilitated the concentrated wealth and power that we see in corporations now, and it has enabled our own democratically enacted laws to be used against us. Thomas Jefferson predicted that the judiciary branch could destroy the democratic Republic he had helped create; he called the U.S. Supreme Court the "engine of consolidation."

Move to Amend is building and coalescing a people's movement to counter and correct the Supreme Court. Our goal is to amend the U.S. Constitution to affirm that only human beings have constitutional rights. We aim to abolish corporate personhood and to rewrite the illegitimate judicial creation that equates money with speech. How are we doing this? It is one thing to go to universities and have this very elite discussion about amending the Constitution, but how are we addressing this cause with the rest of America? We're working from the ground up, and local communities are the primary actors.

People often ask who we are working with in Congress. Forget Congress for now. Congress is broken and the system is broken. Why would we expect a broken system to fix itself? We must turn our backs on the existing power structure and do what the Abolitionists and the Suffragists did. They saw that the power to fix the problems lay within them. We, too, are going to use our power and our passion to create the world we want to live in. We are going to live by *our* ideals, and we'll do it so long, and so hard, and so passionately that we'll drag the existing power structure with us. That is what we have to do.

I have spent 250 or more days per year on the road for the last three years giving a talk called "Protecting What We Love" to students ranging from fifth grade to university age. I tell them we have to figure out what we love first, and then we can build our world—which includes an economy—in a way that protects what we love. Right now our economy is structured to prioritize making money at all costs, which works if you don't have to breathe the air or drink the water. What we need to do is build an economy that sustains and nourishes environmental wealth first. We must account for social wealth, and factor in our relationships with each other, our health, and quality time with our children. Finally, we must either build jobs that create community well-being, or create a jobless culture, like subsistence cultures in Alaska, where the economy is based on bartering, cooperative living, and trading. Who said we had to work for money? You can't eat it or drink it. We need to think outside of the box and talk about regenerative communities.

Universities teach triple bottom-line accounting, which is about building one or more forms of wealth without decreasing the others. Communities talk about living economies, which is also about measuring, creating, and balancing all forms of wealth. It's time to put these ideas into practice by changing minds and changing culture. We need to shake things up and have our voices heard loudly and often. We need to protest what we're opposed to and rally for what we're trying to create.

My personal form of protest is my work educating people about chemical illnesses and treatment in the Gulf. The petrochemical industry has managed to capture and reframe the chemical illnesses in the Gulf as "colds and flu," telling people to take a Tylenol when their bodies are trying to fight chemical poisoning. People are confused about why their headaches or skin rashes or respiratory problems won't go away. The symptoms for chemical illnesses mimic many common symptoms. I'm working with communities to start an epidemiology study across the Gulf, because we can't trust the federal government. I'm working to build a democracy movement in the Deep South. This is about us, We the People, taking back the power and writing our own energy legislation without the fossil fuel industry and the nuclear power industry. We have the power to make this change.

Derrick: In all of the talks that I do around the country, I ask people if they believe we live in a democracy. I ask, "Do you believe that governments take better care of human beings than corporations?" Out of thousands and thousands of people, never has a single person said yes. That's an extraordinary state of affairs. It's extraordinary for us to accept this and at the same time be capable of saying that we live in the greatest democracy in the world. It's utterly insane.

I have seen one example of participatory democracy in action that I love to tell about. I live in far northern California. When you think of far northern California, what is the first plant that comes to mind? The county of Del Norte attempted to reduce the number of marijuana plants that a person can grow for medicinal, personal use. You were allowed to have ninety-nine plants, and some people thought that was excessive. The County Board of Supervisors attempted to reduce the number to six, and I have never in my life heard of such an angry crowd as at this meeting. The Supervisors weren't able to implement this plan. Whenever I get too discouraged— which is quite often—I think about this example of participatory democracy actually working. The Board of Supervisors wouldn't have made it out of the room had they changed it.

Riki: I can add more examples to that. I have been traveling a lot, and I feel like a thread in a crazy quilt—the thread that seams all of these stories together. I've actually gotten more hopeful, being on the road, rather than less hopeful. I have found there are fifth graders who can knowledgably talk about waste biofuels. They know the difference between biofuels and waste biofuels; they know about tidal power and solar power. One fifth grader even explained bio-mimicry. I've seen communities that are involved in transition towns and intentional living with five, six, or ten families who share chores and skills. I've given my talk in thirty-three states, and I've seen that many people are worried about the collapse of industrialized society. I say bring it on—the sooner the better. I see already what's coming up to replace the old society. When a forest burns, does that mean the forest is gone forever? No, new shoots come up. I've met pockets of people who know this in different states around the U.S. and in other countries. There are enough pockets, I think, to pull us all through.

Another example of participatory democracy was the Great Duck-In in Barrow, Alaska. The Migratory Bird Act had been amended so there was to be no spring duck hunting. The Native people in Barrow, which is the northernmost town in America, are locked in ice in spring, when the rest of the birds migrate through the lower forty-eight states. The ducks are their first fresh food after winter. They said the amendment wasn't going to work for them, and they went on hunting. The Fish and Wildlife enforcement came into town and arrested a man who had harvested some ducks. The next day, the entire village of Barrow showed up at the hotel where the Fish and Wildlife representative was staying, each individual with as many ducks as they could hold in their hands; every man, woman, and child. The Fish and Wildlife representative climbed out a back window and was never seen again. That collective act of civil disobedience changed the federal law.

This type of unified action is what needed to happen in the Gulf when, for example, the community of Gulf Shores, Alabama, adopted a policy to suppress film crews on the beaches. The city didn't want the film crews to film the oil, as it would hurt tourism. They made a law that film crews had to get permission to film by buying a license for $255 that allowed them to film thirty days in the future, but not immediately. That really put a chill on documentary film crews. If only four hundred documentary film crews had descended on Gulf Shores the day after the law passed and gotten arrested, perhaps the law would have changed. If one person gets arrested, it's not a newsworthy event. We need to think in terms of masses for protesting and resistance.

Derrick: The head of security—such a nice euphemism—during apartheid South Africa said that the thing they were most afraid of from the African National Congress was not sabotage or even violence, but that they would get a mass of South Africans to stop respecting law and order. He said that no security force in the world can withstand a populace that no longer believes in the legitimacy of law and order as such.

Riki: Yes, and whose law is it? In our country, corporations are driving more and more laws through the Supreme Court for their self-preservation and the protection of their bottom line. I tell fifth graders that sometimes laws are morally wrong, and that makes a law broken; "illegitimate" is too big a word for fifth grade. I remind them that the law once held that black people couldn't vote. Isn't that a bad law to think of now? The little kids say, "Yes, that's bad." Another broken law was the one that prevented women from voting. What did black people and women have to do to fix these broken laws? They had to break them to fix them. After hearing this, one little twelve-year-old girl said she couldn't wait until her first arrest. I have not been kicked out of a school yet for teaching this. Civil disobedience is one of the tools in our toolkit that we were given to hold our democracy, such as it is, in check. Let's pick it up and use it.

There are power point presentations on my website, www. ultimatecivics.org, where you can learn more about the evolution of corporate personhood and the demise of democracy. I'm primarily focused on getting off oil, but I realize we can't end our dependency on coal and fossil fuels as long as the oil industry is writing the laws of the land. It's circular. We need to take back the power of the pen, and that means we need to shake things up—the sooner, the better.

Derrick: I gave a talk in New Mexico a few years ago. It was part of a benefit for an organization that was attempting to keep yet another toxic dump site out of yet another poor community of color. The people in the audience commented that many of the police were actually their neighbors, but still they enforced the laws that were passed by those in distant places to assert the rights of distant corporations over their community. We started to brainstorm about how fun it would be if the police actually enforced local communal standards. We all laughed at that fantasy. Then we talked about what it might be like if we in our communities decided to put together local police forces that would enforce cancer-free zones or oil spill–free zones or rape-free zones, for that matter. Communal enforcement of communal, social norms is an important part of the solution here. We have to decide what we love and then we have to defend it.

Riki: The demise of our democracy has been going on in phases. *Gangs of America* is a great book by Ted Nace that tells what has happened in America in the form of a story. The crux of Nace's story is that there have been three critical phases. The first phase started after we fought a revolution against the British monarchy and its money. For the first one hundred or so years after the Revolutionary

War, people held very tight reins over corporations, controlling them carefully through the state legislatures. Corporations were given privileges, not rights. During the next hundred years, phase two, corporations hammered at the legislative doors, demanding more and more privileges and power. This situation evolved, gradually, into state legislatures handing out rights to corporations. We're in the third phase now, where corporations are not even bothering with state law and federal law. They are just writing transnational trade agreements that undermine democratically enacted state and federal laws. Talk about the power getting removed from the people.

Derrick, your mention of cancer-free zones and corporate laws reminds me of another Gulf story. Under federal law oil waste is considered hazardous waste. After the BP disaster in the Gulf, the waste started accumulating too quickly, and there were not enough hazardous waste sites to dispose of it. So the oil waste was declassified from its status as hazardous waste, and now that oil waste is finding its way into local municipal dumps. Of course, the poor communities were targeted first for waste disposal sites, because the richer communities said, "not in our backyard."

What will happen next, I'm betting based on the *Exxon Valdez* experience, is the great scientific controversy to confuse the public about the extent of the damages. There were two bodies of science that came out of the *Exxon Valdez* oil spill. The non-industry-funded scientists said there was a problem and damage from the oil, and that the recovery of the ecosystem was delayed because of the oil. The industry-funded scientists said everything was happy and fine.

Those two bodies of science were made public in 1993 in completely separate forums. I went to both. At the Exxon-funded forum in Atlanta, Georgia, police officers ringed the rooms because, as they said, they were "expecting trouble from Alaska." There were six of us Alaskans who went down for this. The police were worried and expecting trouble from me, Riki Ott. The mayor of Cordova said, "The only thing Riki Ott will shoot off is her mouth." The upshot of the conference was that the police realized they were on the wrong side. To bring this much longer story to a close, at the end, when the six of us were standing around saying goodbye to each other, the police, who had by now befriended us, came and ringed us once more. They were not threatening us, but listening to us say goodbye to each other. I heard one of them behind me say to another, "I have never seen such a large corporation afraid of such a small group of people." When the people unite and speak with one voice, we are unstoppable.

After the Santa Barbara oil spill in 1969, twenty million people in the nation rose up and said we would not accept as "normal" corporations poisoning our oceans, rivers, air, and land for their profit. People wanted more environmental protection, and law after law got passed to protect the environment and public health. Nixon even created the Environmental Protection Agency—which has since been captured, but never mind that.

That level of public outrage and solidarity cannot be tolerated by corporate America. That is why there was and still is such a stomping down of imagery from the Gulf to control the story of damages. There are a lot of sick people in the Gulf, and their story is not going away. It might be suffocated for political reasons, but that story is going to pop out again, because there are too many people in the Gulf who saw what was really going on. I am hopeful that what happened in the Gulf can become the turning point in our national transition to a saner energy future, but it's going to take all of us in America knowing what is going on in the Gulf. Together, we must say: it's time for an energy transition, period.

Postscript: In March 2012, BP and the plaintiffs' committee announced an economic settlement and a medical settlement. The medical settlement contains hundreds of millions of dollars for medical claims, medical monitoring, and medical services including five community health care clinics across the Gulf, staffed with doctors trained to treat chemical illnesses.

This is the first time human health impacts have been recognized in an oil spill. Even though the medical settlement looks good on paper, it contains many, many details that could easily limit BP's liability as to how much the corporation will have to pay injured people. In addition to limiting its medical liability, BP is claiming that wildlife in the Gulf is thriving and more abundant since the disaster. Exxon claimed this as well, the year following the spill. Wildlife in Prince William Sound still has not recovered; the herring fisheries are closed indefinitely until stocks recover. I expect this story of long-term harm to repeat in the Gulf.

Riki Ott, June 11, 2012

Nora Barrows-Friedman

"Dominant culture, in terms of the industry of colonialism in Palestine, is exactly the same as it was here in the Americas. The Zionist narrative that has been invented, the idea that the Jews are the only 'chosen people' for this land and everyone else is just in the way, is the manifest destiny of reasoning that was actually established here five hundred years ago."

Derrick Jensen: Nora Barrows-Friedman is an award-winning journalist who focuses on colonialism in Palestine.

Nora, what are some of the patterns and examples of the dominant culture's paradigm that are revealed in a place like Palestine, and what are the similarities we see on this continent?

Every day, when I read about new so-called settlements, I can't help but think that I could have been reading newspapers 130 years ago or 180 years ago about that happening in Native North America—that process of the dominant population saying they are only going to take a little piece of ground, and then continuing to take more.

Nora Barrows-Friedman: Palestine's situation is like a carbon copy of what has been happening on this continent for so many hundreds of years. In a place like Palestine, political and environmental colonialism merges. There isn't oil underneath the ground in Palestine, but there is water, for example. It's also a regional access point for Western imperialist powers to launch various wars of aggression, or to store massive amounts of weapons, or to secretly produce nuclear weapons. To have an operating base, a client state in that part of the world for the U.S. and for Europe to use, is part of the political context.

Then there's an environmental context. Israelis are a settler-colonialist society, and the Indigenous people have been pushed into ghettos surrounded by imperialist forces. The physical structures of the settlements are some of the clearest examples of this paradigm. There are over 140 actual settlement blocs inside the occupied West Bank, and hundreds of what we call "outposts," which are extensions of these settlement blocs, and which eventually connect with other settlement blocs. It looks like a spreading cancer all over the West Bank. Now communities are completely cut off from each other and the tops of the hillsides have literally been chopped.

There's a hill I'm thinking about, just outside of Bethlehem, where I'm based when I'm in Palestine. This hillside was a nature preserve for generations and generations, and it was one of the most sacred spaces for Palestinians. There were trees, flora, and fauna that were endemic only to this hillside for so long. No one tried to change it; people went to have picnics and to celebrate the land.

Before and during 1948, three-quarters of a million Palestinians were purged, and the settler-colonial state was established as Israel. Subsequently, the occupations came, and after 1967, the settlements started popping up over the occupied West Bank including East Jerusalem.

The top of this hillside was sheared off. All of the trees were cut down, and you can't find one tree on this hillside anymore. A fortress went up.

There are books about the architecture of occupation, the architecture of settler-colonialism. You would think that these settlers, after "winning the land," land they say they are attached to, would act in concert with the land and build structures designed to preserve its natural state. But this is not the case, and because it's such a militarized system, the structures that they've built look like actual fortresses, and are completely antithetical to the landscape. They sheared off the top of the hill and built square, massive, ten-story homes and apartment buildings. They ringed them around what is left of the hillside so densely that you can't see any land in between the houses. They look down upon the Palestinian villages and valleys below.

The psychology of that is not lost on the people whose land that once was, and still is. The Indigenous are not only watching their land being erased and turned into military fortresses of power and colonialism, but they are also seeing the fortresses as forbidding and startling images. They are being surrounded by them. There are entire villages that are surrounded on all sides by fortresses and by people who want to erase the Palestinians.

Derrick: Let's go back to the phrase "dominant cultural paradigm" that I mentioned in the first question. What is that?

Nora: Dominant culture, in terms of the industry of colonialism in Palestine, is exactly the same as it was here in the Americas. The Zionist narrative that has been invented, the idea that the Jews are the only "chosen people" for this land and everyone else is just in the way, is the manifest destiny of reasoning that was actually established here five hundred years ago. It's intrinsic to how we feel about this place and what our children are taught about this place.

My daughter, who's about to be ten years old, goes to a fantastic school in Oakland that is very social justice–oriented, but she is still exposed to channels of the dominant culture narrative that are endemic to American education. She's learning now about the gold rush, and I chaperoned a field trip during which we learned about the history of how California was founded on a capitalist land grab and resource theft. This is just like what's happening in Palestine, where land is being gobbled up by foreigners.

But before the field trip, my daughter came home with a couple pages of lyrics from songs she had been learning in class. I wrote down some of the lyrics. One goes, "That gold was here for me to find." Another goes, "I got the itch to strike it rich." I was shocked that this is still the narrative that is being promoted, even in a school that is social justice–oriented. This dominant culture narrative is like a poison, and it is almost impossible to dislocate it from our lives, from the stories of our history.

I talked to my daughter about this. I said that we really need to understand what it means to say "this gold was here for me to find." Whose gold is it? In Iraq, why is "our" oil under their sand? Why is Israel—historic Palestine—a land for just one people, because it says so in a book that someone wrote, as if God was a real-estate agent? Why do we still accept these narratives, and why is the dominant culture a culture that is built on destruction, death, violence, and taking without giving? Why are we still putting up with this?

I go to Palestine and see these hillsides being chopped to pieces and Israeli settlers attacking children. The theft of land by settlers is supposedly acceptable, but to fight back against the dominant cultural paradigm becomes incomprehensible, in the same way that it is incomprehensible for Native people here to fight back against the continued theft of their land and the continued marginalization of their communities. They are supposed to be happy with what they've been given.

Derrick: How does the colonial structure affect people's connection with the landbase? I think we have a few different sets of people to talk about here: the colonizer settlers, the disposed, and those who remain but are subjugated.

Nora: For the settlers who are taking that land by violent force, fueled by a supremacist perversion of a religious belief system, I think it has turned from a relationship of guardianship of the land—this mystical, biblical attachment—to a militant possessive quality of ownership. Settlers are now mandated to carry weapons with them. They have the state's military forces at their behest. They are encouraged by the state that has driven these policies into entrenchment and allowed them to take over Palestinian homes in East Jerusalem on a regular basis.

This has, in fact, disconnected the settlers as a community—I'm being generous—from their relationship with and love for the land. For them, the land is a commodity with which to solidify their hierarchy and supremacy. They feel entitled to cut off the top of a mountain and dry up rivers to make fortress-like structures.

For the people who have been dispossessed from that land for the last six-and-a-half decades—there are now seven million disposed Palestinians in the global diaspora, which is the largest refugee community in the world and in modern history—it has become a mythical place. Palestinians who haven't been back since 1948, or those who live in the U.S., talk about their land this way. I've done countless interviews and oral history projects with people living in refugee camps that are literally twenty minutes away from their ancestral land, which is now in ruins or has been turned into some kind of Israeli community. They go off in their imagination, as though they were there, and they still remember what their house looked like, and where they turned on a certain road to get bread from a baker, and what the school looked like, the smell of the trees in the fall. There were 531 villages that were destroyed from 1948 to 1952, but the ghosts and memories of those villages are still alive.

The oldest generation remembers these things very personally and vividly. It's heart-wrenching to talk to them. I remember a conversation I had with an elder in a refugee camp who is now in his eighties; he said, "All I want to do is die and have my bones buried in my land." He knew that his land—in a village just twenty minutes away from where he was standing—was now under the heap of a huge forest that was planted by the Jewish National Fund. In 1948, this greenwashing industry came in to literally erase and cover up the crimes of the colonial project. The elder knew that he would not recognize the land if he were there today. It has become a collective figment of imagination. But for the people who are living under that subjugation, this mythical land is a major driving force in why they still are there and why they haven't left yet.

Derrick: I interviewed Vine Deloria Jr. about ten years ago, and he said that it is a crucial time for the Plains Indians because many of the last of the people who were born unconquered, undisposed—born free, as he put it—died in the 1930s. So, the last people that had ever spoken to the people who had been born free were still alive. I'm thinking about that as you speak of the older people who were living twenty miles away from their land.

Nora: Indigenous communities all over the world have a special relationship to the land. I think the colonizers have seen that a sign of weakness; if you have an intrinsic romance with the land, then you are easily conquerable.

The older generation of Palestinians with whom I've spoken are the most unconquered people. They were the ones who walked—not drove—with all of their possessions on their backs for miles and days. Some of them went to Lebanon and Syria and Jordan. Some ended up in Gaza or the West Bank. Many of them went overseas. They were driven out, and yet they are exactly the same people who they were six decades ago, with the same attachment to the land. It was that way with the old man who was speaking about just wanting for his bones to be buried with his land. There's such reverence in that.

There's a way in which the resilience was underestimated by the colonizers. The early colonizers of the 1940s thought that they could drive everyone out and the Palestinians would find somewhere else to live and be happy in another Arab country. This is still said. They underestimated the stubbornness of that attachment to the land, and the stubbornness of people who still have that history inside of them. You can find that here or anywhere in the world.

Derrick: How do people resist? Is resistance possible?

Nora: In that stubbornness, in not giving up and not giving in, there's resistance. There's a great line in this documentary that I recently saw about Gaza. It was made in the days after the massacres in 2008 and 2009, when 1,400 Palestinians, including about 400 children, were killed in a twenty-two-day bombing strike. The filmmaker interviewed a man who was a farmer. His strawberry and wheat field had been completely obliterated by bombs, and was still riddled with landmines, so he couldn't enter. He looked at his field and said, "I'd love to feed all who inhabit this earth. I make soldiers out of wheat stalks." That is particularly poignant, and it's reflective of how his people have been able to survive. Inherent in that sentiment is a relationship with the land. The land itself is part of the resistance.

I mentioned the trees that the Jewish National Fund planted to cover up the crimes of the ethnic cleansing program. The whole thing is such a huge metaphor. They came over on boats with these trees, and they planted them. Some of them were pine and cypress trees imported from other Mediterranean countries, so they weren't native species. Here in the U.S. you can "plant a tree for Israel." It was a greenwashing, environmentally focused industry to move the Native people and native species out. Well, these trees, now sixty-odd years old, are suffering a major disease problem, because they are not an endemic species. They are dying out, and the old endemic species are coming back in and taking over some of the forests again. For example, a cactus species native to the Mediterranean coast is now coming back up. Before the settler-colonialism era, Palestinian farmers used to delineate their farms with these cacti, representing boundaries and borders for livestock.

There's a lot of solace in this. I think we forget that nature is also going to take care of the land, too. These species which were intended to be wiped out are also stubborn—as stubborn as the people. That's resistance.

The political and militant resistance in Palestinian society has tried everything. Some of it has worked; some of it has not worked. People aren't ready to give up either way. A lot of people are being tenacious and trying to learn as much as they can about previous struggles around the world. A good friend of mine who is twenty-three years old—and absolutely brilliant—is an expert on Algerian resistance, and an expert on Native resistance in the U.S. I think resistance also has a lot to do with stubbornness, and I think we have a lot to learn about that.

Derrick: I was talking to a technotopian who was saying that people all over the world want to live the way people in the United States live, with computers, iPods, and cell phones. We have basically everything we want except a cancer-free existence on a living planet. He was actually pushing the "White Man's Burden."

Looking at things this way, what are the Palestinians complaining about? Aren't Israelis bringing in industry and jobs, and don't they actually improve the standard of living?

Nora: We call this the "happy slave" mentality. Industrialized capitalism is all about promoting the idea that your life could be better if you had these things. Palestinians are meant to believe that their lives are better now because they can get a permission slip from the Israeli government saying that they can work inside an Israeli settlement and provide food for their family. The dominant narrative says that the Jewish, Zionist colonists "made the desert bloom," as though the Zionists came to an empty, barren place. They supposedly brought industry and agriculture techniques to a people with no idea how to grow vegetables. Aren't they so lucky?

Today, there are clear systems of apartheid and legalized inequality between Jewish Israelis and everyone else. The rest of the world may be placated by the fact that Palestinian citizens of Israel—who now make up 20 percent of the population—get to vote and hold public office. Sure, they don't have the same public school system, and they don't get the same water resources, and they don't get the same privileges that the Jewish Israeli community has, but, the narrative goes, we'll let them have their communities and let them have their public offices. Aren't they lucky? What are they complaining about?

It's the same here in the United States. We have our iPods. Sure, we get cancer and our seas have been poisoned for the rest of our lives, and for our grandchildren's lives, and for their grandchildren's lives, but we get cars. We should thank the industrial capitalists.

Derrick: This is a very old narrative, and it's certainly biblical. In North America there's a great line by Captain John Chester, who said that the Natives would receive "the riches of our faith," while the Europeans would take the materials of the forest. A proslavery philosopher from 1830 wrote of how the slaves were actually ennobled by their contact with the superior minds of the slave owners. If we could, I would really like to try to debunk that. We can both make fun of it, but the fact is that within a capitalist, colonialist structure—and insofar as you've been colonized by the capitalist, colonialist mindset—that does become what you value. One of the ways I've put this in one of my books—which doesn't debunk it, but continues to make fun of it—is that if I'm going to be in a prison, I'd rather be a trustee than one of the lower-level prisoners. I'd rather not be in a prison at all, unless it's got some good cars and nice health care.

Nora: I think that's debunked every day, actually. I think in Palestine it's debunked by the fact that there are more than fifty refugee camps, and these refugee camps are not paradises. In one camp in Bethlehem that I've had as a base since 2005, there are twelve thousand people in half of a square kilometer. People are packed. They're living on top of each other. If your neighbor sneezes, the guy across the street, ten houses down, can hear. There's no privacy. Everyone is in each other's business. There are no places for children to play. The Israeli military comes in every single night and rounds people up. There were—up until just a few years ago—open trench sewers. Between 1948 and 1953, everyone lived in canvas tents. From 1953 until the mid-1970s, people were in asbestos-filled eight-by-eight shacks, where there were twenty families to one bathroom. Now, it's like a huge city.

The twelve thousand people in that one refugee camp are living in some of the worst conditions in the world, while just twenty minutes across the green line, people who happen to have been born Jewish are living in the lap of luxury, with their swimming pools and upscale settlements. But when you go into the refugee camp and ask people their names and where they are from, they don't say the name of the refugee camp. They tell you the specific village from which their families were expelled. A two-year-old kid knows where his great-grandparents were born. That is a tool against the colonialist structure.

A friend of mine, for example, has to go to the American Consulate in East Jerusalem to get her passport in order to leave the country. But to go to the American Consulate in East Jerusalem, she's first supposed to go to the Israeli District Coordinating Office in the adjacent settlement colony bloc near Bethlehem, where she is to apply for permission to leave Bethlehem to go across the checkpoint to go to Jerusalem to get her passport to leave the country. She has decided for the last six years not to get permission. Instead, she finds ways to get across that checkpoint without having to appeal for permission from the colonizers who hold an illogical, bureaucratic stranglehold of control over her people. She, as a measure of her own tenacity, militantly refuses to be subjugated by a piece of paper that dictates when she can go to her land, which is right next to Jerusalem, and to which her parents can't go. By refusing to be part of that system, she refuses the tenets of colonialism.

Derrick: How does that apply to us?

Nora: We have to be willing to take responsibility. I, for example, as a 100 percent Jewish woman, who has an American passport and has U.S. citizenship, have, by this ridiculous accident of birth, become a very privileged person when I go to Palestine. I don't get searched at the airport. I don't get harassed and detained at checkpoints. I show my passport and I'm let through wherever I go. This is a privilege I didn't ask for, but which has become a tool now for conveying information about what's happening on the ground there to people elsewhere. As a Jewish-American passport holder in Palestine, I needn't cry about my privilege, because what tangible good does that do?

Those of us who have privilege can be vehicles for information exchange, and, as a preschool teacher once said to my daughter, we can use our powers for good. We can't be consumed with the "White Man's Burden" and guilt, because they just weigh on us pointlessly. Instead, we can use the accident of our birth to create good change in this world, and to inform other people about what's happening. That's the responsibility we have.

Derrick: As a white man, I've thought about this quite a bit. Part of my responsibility as someone with utter privilege is to use this privilege to undercut its basis.

Nora: If we give our guilt so much power, it just builds it up even more.

Derrick: Journalists are always told to tell "both sides" of a story and to be objective. The point I try to make again and again in *Endgame* is that all writing is propaganda. How does this fit into your work?

Nora: I think language is incredibly important, and especially so in covering a story like Palestine or covering stories like the BP disaster. This myth of objectivity is such a disservice to people. As you said, we are inherently biased because we are human beings and we feel and have opinions, and that goes for journalists, too. I've seen so many journalists who are stenographers. That's all they do; they are stenographers for the dominant culture, because they feel that's the platform that we should all aspire to, as information disseminators.

Journalists, writers, thinkers, philosophers, and educators have been told to present both sides when they're talking about important situations. But everyone knows about Israel's struggle and its pain and suffering. Nobody knows about the causality of that narrative and what Palestinians have been struggling against. When we are asked or tasked with this notion that, to be a professional journalist or to be a good writer, you should present both sides, that's incredibly destructive, actually. There is a motive and objective within the dominant culture to uphold the status quo, which is one of destruction and killing and violence and uprootedness of culture. Presenting this side of the story helps keep the structures of capitalism and imperialism in place.

Take Gaza, for example, where an economic blockade was enacted as a collective punishment for choosing the wrong party in one of the most free and fair democratic elections in the Middle East in decades. There was a list of banned items. At the top of the list of banned medications to Gaza was anesthesia. Therefore, it was made a *policy* that the Palestinians should feel as much pain as possible for choosing the wrong people in a free and fair democratic election. This was not a metaphor or hyperbole, but an actual policy that doctors could not guarantee pain-free surgeries.

Think of a journalist going to that hospital and witnessing what was happening, seeing people come in after bombs had been dropped on them and endure surgeries without anesthesia. Imagine the journalist writing that "the Israeli military said there was a target, so they had no choice but to bomb it." What a disservice that would be. What a way to be completely unaccountable to the people about whom the journalist was reporting.

When we write and we educate, we have to think about who we're being accountable to. In journalism—especially wartime journalism—the people who are the ones under the thumb of an occupation or regime or violent, militaristic paradigm and policies are the ones toward whom writers undoubtedly should be accountable. They are the ones from whom we're not hearing, and they are the ones who are made into subhumans and demons so that we don't feel anything for them.

Here's a story from the bombings in Gaza. There's a zoo in the southernmost part of the Gaza strip. The Israelis bombed the zoo while it was full of animals. The birds left, and for months afterward my friends said that there were no birds in the trees in Gaza. But the ostriches and a lion or two who were seen running through the streets of Rafah after the bombing. They didn't have wings and couldn't fly out, and eventually they died.

If we're not accountable to the people, plants, and animals who are asking us to recognize them and their stories, then we've done an incredible disservice to this planet. As collective members of this world, we must believe that we can change something.

Gail Dines

"People often say to me,
isn't pornography fantasy?
Fantasy happens in the head;
pornography happens in the
international banks of capitalism.
That's not fantasy, that's
economics."

Derrick Jensen: Dr. Gail Dines has been described as the world's leading antipornography campaigner. She is a professor of sociology and women's studies at Wheelock College in Boston, and her writing and lectures focus on the ways that porn images filter into mainstream pop culture.

Gail Dines: When I speak about porn, people often have an image in their head of *Playboy* from fifteen years ago: a naked woman coyly smiling in a cornfield. That was bad enough, because it commodified and sexualized women. But pornography today is so hardcore that it is absolutely unrecognizable when compared to what it was a generation ago. That's because of the internet, which made pornography affordable, accessible, and anonymous, the three factors that really increase consumption. There is now an increasing market for an increasingly violent set of images. Studies show that the age when boys first view pornography is eleven years old. All of this means that there are now a lot of men and boys viewing a lot of violent pornography.

Just think about how it was a generation ago. When a fourteen-year-old boy, with hormones raging, wanted to look at pornography, he had to go find his father's *Playboy*. He had limited access to these images. Now, think about how things are today: boys have complete access to porn twenty-four/seven. In addition, today's pornographic images are no longer softcore. In fact, softcore pornography has migrated into pop culture. What we are left with, on the internet, is body-punishing, cruel, abusive, violent sex. Many of these images would not look out of place on an Amnesty International website. They depict sexual cruelty and torture.

People think they know what this pornography looks like, but until you've seen it, your imagination cannot begin to know what it really shows. I'll give two examples. One of the main acts now in pornography is gagging; the man puts his penis so far down the woman's throat that she gags, sometimes to the point of vomiting. That's now commonplace. The second thing that's very popular is what is called ATM, or ass-to-mouth. This is where the man puts his penis into the woman's anus and then straight into her mouth without washing. What they are finding now is that women are suffering from fecal bacterial infections of the throat. This is a whole new level of debasement and dehumanization, because sex in pornography is designed to debase and dehumanize. Indeed, the more you can debase, the greater the sizzle.

We need to be worried about this. We're bringing up a generation of boys as sexual sadists. This is a major public health issue of our time.

Derrick: One of the central ideas of a "spectacle" is that it always has to get worse, because there is no emotional involvement. We saw it with the coliseum in Rome and we certainly see it today. I recently saw about ten minutes of the movie *Hostel II*, and in the first scene I watched, a woman was tied upside down over a bathtub, naked and bleeding, as a second naked woman bathed in her blood. Thirty or forty years ago, this would presumably be considered pretty outrageous, even for hardcore pornography. Now, it's in a major money-making film.

Gail: I think what is key to all of this is the desensitization of the individual and the culture. What we can tolerate now as a culture is completely different from what we could tolerate a generation ago. Indeed, what study after study shows is that the more violence in pornography men see, the greater the need for increased levels of violence to keep them interested and aroused. This didn't happen by accident. Men do not wake up one day and think that they want to watch a woman being gagged. What the pornographers do, together with their buddies in pop culture, is socialize men into this pattern. Taste, in terms of media, is socialized. It's not something inherent. What we have done in our culture is basically condition men to want really violent porn. Movies like *Hostel II* are precursors to the porn world, as is Grand Theft Auto, which is one of the best-selling video games. In that game, you get points for killing prostitutes. You kill them in the most vile, hateful ways imaginable.

Just imagine this: you're brought up on a steady diet of movies like *Hostel II*, games like Grand Theft Auto, and MTV. What are you going to want in your pornography? The old centerfold images aren't going to do much for you. That's why *Playboy* magazine is going bankrupt. The only thing *Playboy* can manage to make money on now is its branding. *Penthouse* went bankrupt years ago. *Hustler* is only in business because of its websites. What used to be the unholy trinity of porn, *Playboy*, *Penthouse*, and *Hustler*, basically no longer exists, because who wants it?

Derrick: What does it mean for boys and men to grow up in this century with pornography?

Gail: For most boys today, pornography is the major form of sex education. It is the most powerful form of sex education because pornography sends messages to men's brains via the penis, which is an incredibly powerful delivery system. What it means is that boys become habituated to images of debasement and dehumanization, and the more habituated they become, the more they internalize those images into their sexual template.

What I have found—and what studies have found—in interviews with men is that, first of all, they internalize the porn-world image. They think that people are behaving the way they see people behave in porn. There was a preliminary study done at NYU, in which men were asked what was the one sex act that they'd never done and would love to do, and 80 percent said it was to ejaculate on a woman's face. Now, where did they get that idea? It's straight out of pornography. Nobody thinks that up by themselves. What men are increasingly doing is having porn sex with their girlfriends. Much to my sadness, a lot of the women are capitulating. They're not negotiating with men, but capitulating to them.

Pornography is industrial-strength sex. It's the industrialization and commodification of sex. People get used to masturbating to a hardcore level of imagery, and sex with a real human being no longer cuts it. I've had many men tell me how they are disinterested in sex with their girlfriends. One guy told me that when he has sex with his girlfriend he tries to do it as quickly as possible, so she'll leave and he can get to the pornography. Another thing they tell me is that in order to ejaculate, they have to pull up the images of pornography, because they are no longer interested in their girlfriends, who don't look like the well-oiled, big-breasted porn performers.

This has filtered down into college campuses today in the form of hook-up sex culture. Studies are showing that dating is increasingly becoming a thing of the past because of hook-up sex. Hook-up sex can be anything from kissing to intercourse, but no matter what it is, nobody expects a relationship to develop—unless you can call a series of hook-ups with the same person a relationship. Studies have shown that women participate in hook-up sex because they hope a more intimate relationship is going to come of it. Of course this doesn't happen. Hook-up sex is porn sex; it is sex with no connection, no intimacy, no feelings, and no emotions one associates with love, empathy, or kindness. Boys and men are internalizing the value system of pornography.

Derrick: You mention in your book, *Pornland*, that Hugh Hefner, according to one of his ex-girlfriends, will penetrate various women, but can only ejaculate to porn.

Gail: What this young woman said is that Hugh Hefner lines up his "girlfriends," who you may know about from the TV show *The Girls Next Door*, which is a glamorization of Hefner's life with working-class, eighteen-year-old girls competing with one another for his attention. Hefner then coats himself in baby oil and has sex with each one, one after another. The baby oil causes all sorts of vaginal infections, but he keeps doing it. He uses no protection, either. When he's done, he sends them all away and turns on his pornography and masturbates to ejaculation. It's the only way he can do it.

Playboy was crucial. People say that there's always been pornography, so what's new? But the pornography *industry* only started in 1953 with the first edition of *Playboy*. Why? Because, it was the first time that porn images were circulated through the channels of mainstream American capitalism.

How is it possible that in 1953, probably the most conservative decade of the century, *Playboy* became an overnight success? To understand this, you have to understand what capitalist America needed after the Second World War. Europe was in ruins, and they wanted to build this country up as a major superpower. To build a superpower up, they needed people willing to spend money. In order to spend money, people needed to buy on credit, but the emerging middle class was a generation of men and women who were brought up during a war and a depression; these were frugal people.

In came the media industry. It's no accident that 1950 saw the massive expansion in the number of televisions sold. People had been living in tenement blocks, in multifamily homes. Suddenly, they were moved to the suburbs, and many didn't even know how to furnish a house there. I know it sounds ridiculous to say that people didn't know how to consume, but it was true in the fifties. The sitcoms were brought in, and by showing all the rooms in a typical suburban house, they trained American women about what to buy. In fact, one of the reasons that the "ranch house" was developed was because homes only had one TV. They wanted women to be able to watch TV, but women were often in the kitchen. So, developers designed a house layout that allowed people to see from the kitchen into the living room. It was that well organized.

Sitcoms like *Leave It to Beaver* and *Father Knows Best* taught women how to consume, but the men also needed training. This is where Hefner hit on a brilliant idea. *Playboy* became the consumer training manual for men. The basic message in *Playboy* was this: if you consume at the level that we tell you to consume, then you will get the real prize, which is the women in the magazine, or women who look like the ones in the magazine. Remember, Hefner loves the term "the girl next door." With *Playboy*, this was crucial, because he had to get readers to believe that they could get girls like this, that they were real.

In the first editions of *Playboy*, there were very few images of women, but there were articles about what suit to wear or what desk to buy. It was all about how to buy products. What Hefner did there was very smart, because he did not just commodify sexuality; he also sexualized commodities. That's the best way to sell things. Once the advertisers realized that *Playboy* was providing an identity based on consumption for the upwardly mobile white male, they overcame their squeamishness about advertising in a porn magazine.

Playboy ran the show until 1969, when the *Chicago Tribune* ran a full-page ad showing the *Playboy* bunny in the crosshairs of a rifle. Underneath, it said, "we're going bunny hunting." It was an advertisement for *Penthouse*. Between 1969 and 1973, there was a war between *Penthouse* and *Playboy* to see who could create the most explicit imagery. What's interesting is that *Penthouse* won the battle, but *Playboy* won the war, because *Penthouse* became so explicit that all the advertisers left and ran back to *Playboy*. That war between 1969 and 1973 opened the doors for mainstream porn to become more hardcore. It's no accident that in 1973, a strip club owner from Ohio, Larry Flynt, started *Hustler* magazine. *Playboy* and *Penthouse* laid the groundwork for *Hustler*, and these three magazines laid the cultural, economic, and legal groundwork for the present-day multi-billion-dollar-per-year industry.

From its very beginnings, *Playboy* was totally folded into the dictates of American capitalism. People often say to me, isn't pornography fantasy? Fantasy happens in the head; pornography happens in the international banks of capitalism. That's not fantasy, that's economics.

Derrick: We've talked a lot about men. What does this mean for girls and women? We should also include the fact that boys are abused.

Gail: Boys who are abused are the missing victims from much of the debate. Violence perpetrated against boys is mostly done by men, and we offer too few services that deal with the trauma that comes from sexual abuse.

Derrick: They are made into inferior Others. They are sexually feminized.

Gail: Yes, that's what you do to little boys; you feminize them. They say that a lot of pedophiles will rape a boy or a girl until puberty. They are equal opportunity abusers.

In terms of what it means for girls, just imagine what it is like today to grow up in a world where your role models are Britney, Paris, Miley, Rihanna, and Lindsay. I don't even need to say their last names. Imagine what that's like to live in this hypersexualized image-based culture when you are an adolescent in the process of building your gender and sexual identity. The way you build that identity is by wandering through the culture, looking for cues for what it means to be male or what it means to be female. As an adolescent girl, the only cues you have coming at you are the Paris Hilton–style images. You look through *Cosmopolitan*, you turn on MTV, you watch the

Kardashians—wherever you look, what you see is this hypersexualized example of what you're supposed to become.

For many girls, these images are their only examples of femininity. Girls are surrounded by peers wearing the low-slung jeans, the "tramp stamp" (which is what they call a tattoo on the back; it's worn with a thong, so it is revealed when one bends down), the pierced belly button, and the low-cut top. What happens to girls who choose not to look like that? Well, women in this patriarchy are basically divided into two: you're either fuckable or you're invisible. You tell me what adolescent girl wants to be invisible. They believe that no guy is going to look at them if they're not hypersexualized.

This culture has become a collective perpetrator. We have a perp-culture. We used to have individual rapists or pedophiles who would groom individual boys or girls, and what we now have is an entire culture grooming an entire generation of girls to give men what they want sexually.

I interviewed seven men in prison, all of whom were in for downloading child pornography. Not one of them was a pedophile. Can you get your head around that? Increasingly, men who prefer sex with adult women are getting bored with pornography of adult women and are trying child pornography for a change. The men I interviewed were all in their forties. One of them looked at me and said that this culture groomed his ten-year-old daughter for him. He's absolutely right. He never took a course in women's studies or media studies, but he got it completely right.

There's a study by the American Psychological Association that shows that the more hypersexualized a girl is, the more she experiences depression, anxiety, drug abuse, alcohol abuse, and low selfesteem. Those are exactly the signs people exhibit if they have been raped. We're bringing up a generation of girls who act as if they'd been raped, but haven't actually been raped. That's not to belittle what actual rape is—not at all, because it's more traumatic.

My female students have capitulated to men's sexual demands. They have given in. One of the reasons for this is that we now have so-called "Third Wave Feminism," which is basically Feminism Lite, a kind of feminism without politics. Women are told that it is empowering to be in the porn culture, empowering to be a stripper, and empowering to have as much sex as you want with men. The feminist movement has totally bought into that ideology.

Derrick: Let's go back to the question of capitalism. How does pornography intersect with the other capitalist industries? Isn't it just a few perverts who make a lot of money?

Gail: If only. Many, many men now are making a fortune.

I went to the porn expo in Las Vegas, which is where thousands of porn fans travel to hang out with their favorite pornographers and porn performers. I went to the industry workshops, and what's interesting is that not one person there talked about sex; they talked about money. There was a whole workshop on whether bulk mailing is better than e-mail. Money is what gets pornographers aroused and excited. Pornography is absolutely, at its core, a capitalist industry, and it intersects with many other industries to maximize profit.

Take the credit card companies, for example. Now pornography is purchased online with a credit card. Pornography also intersects with the hotel industry, which makes about half a billion dollars from porn; more money than it makes from the in-room bars. Pornography intersects with the real estate industry in California, especially, because the bulk of porn is made in the valley. It intersects with the mainstream media industry, because two of the big distributors of pornography are Comcast and DirecTV, which are owned by major corporations. At one time the person who made the most money from pornography was Rupert Murdoch, because he owned DirectTV, which was distributing more pornography than any other company. This is how porn intersects with other industries. There's no more a predatory capitalist than Rupert Murdoch.

Because pornographers are in bed economically with mainstream industry, it encourages mainstream industry to facilitate a glamourized image of pornography. For example, Oprah Winfrey had porn star Jenna Jameson on her show. Jameson has moved seamlessly from pornography to pop culture and back again, and Oprah took the cameras to Jameson's house to show the audience her private art collection, beautiful home, and expensive cars.

Imagine that you saw that episode of *Oprah* as a working-class girl working minimum-wage jobs. Jenna's path would certainly look like a viable alternative to Walmart, especially with wholesome Oprah's endorsement. Cleverly placed porn stars who have made a fortune have young women thinking that they can be the next Jenna Jameson. In reality, the average young woman has a shelf life of three months in the porn industry. Most women's bodies cannot tolerate the violence they are subjected to. They are lucky if they leave with the clothes on their backs, and many end up in the brothels of Nevada. That's the reality of women in pornography, contrary to Oprah Winfrey's hideous representation.

Derrick: What role does the mass media play in getting people to accept the corporate interests as their own?

Gail: You know, what's so amazing about Karl Marx is that he could tell the future. The model he constructed argues that the economic base (i.e., capitalism, in this case) determines and shapes all the other institutions of society—education, media, government, religion. Capitalists have to get control of these institutions in order to legitimize why 1 percent of the population owns everything. They have to construct a story to explain this ridiculousness, and the role of the media is to help them do that.

I have a fabulous class this semester. We have discussed racism from a radical perspective. They are interested in discussing Marxism, gender, you name it. Do you know what they fought me about, tooth and nail? Disney. We talked about Disney as a corporate predator, and they were absolutely furious with me. They told me that when I attack Disney, I'm attacking their childhood. That's the role Disney plays. Disney represents what Americans would like to think America really is: innocent.

The media brainwashes us and fills our heads with trivial stuff. On the first day of class, I said to my students, how many of you know that Brad left Jen for Angelina? All of their hands went up. I then asked, how many of you know about the Kyoto agreement? Not one hand up. The media also tells you that you are what you consume; that without your products, you don't have an identity.

Derrick: This reminds me of a great line by Henry Adams: "The press is the hired agent of a moneyed system, set up for no other reason than to tell lies where the interests are concerned."

As long as you're going to go after Disney, let's go after a different sacred cow. In the 1970s, it used to be fun to make fun of the Soviet Politburo for being 97 percent Communist Party members, saying the elections were fake and it wasn't a democracy. Now, in the United States, what percentage of the House of Representatives and the Senate would you say are capitalist party members?

Gail: 100 percent. There's no such thing as democracy in capitalism. You can't have it.

Have you heard of Anthony Wedgwood Benn? He was a very left-wing British politician. He was interviewed by CNN a number of years ago, by the usual CNN interviewer with big hair and a well-toned body. She said to Anthony Benn something like, "Now that Russia is no longer Communist and is democratic . . ." He said, no, Russia is not democratic. She went on, "Now that it is democratic and communism is gone . . ." He said, no it's not: you can't have capitalism and democracy. She didn't have a framework to understand what he was saying.

Benn was exactly right, in that you cannot have a capitalist economy and democracy. Capitalism does not allow democracy; how can it? If you allow real democracy, the average person is going to vote out the elites. A lot of these people are themselves not wealthy, but they vote for the very people who exploit them.

Here's a conversation I have with my students. I say, if I want to be president tomorrow, what do I need? Money, they all say. I say, okay, so I need lots and lots of money, like $80 million just to start the campaign. So, where do I go? I go to the capitalists. I go to GE and I tell them I really want to run for president. GE asks what I can do for them. I say that I'm going to establish an international tribunal court, because GE has created more superfund sites than anyone else, and they're going on trial. I doubt GE will be giving me much money. Or I go to Disney and tell them that they, too, are going on trial for the destruction of children's culture. Of course, they are not going to give me any money. So, I say to my students, before you even listen to any candidate, what you know without question is they have been bought. In an election you decide which corporation you want in power, but ultimately it makes no difference, because they all have the same vested interest in capitalism.

Derrick: Can there be a Left, when there is not a strong anticapitalist movement?

Gail: I grew up with a Left. I do remember when there was a Left. As a radical feminist, I have a very uneasy relationship with the Left today, as most radical feminists do. The first reason is that the Left has embraced pornography and refuses to come out against it. I say in my book that as left-wingers, we have completely agreed that the media is a tool of the capitalists. We completely understand that Fox manipulates and molds its viewers, and seduces them. So why, when we understand that, do we suddenly decide that porn is the only media product that has no effect? Fox can manipulate and seduce, but not pornography; that's completely different. What the Left has done is refuse to take on pornography.

I wrote an article with Bob Jensen called, "Why Pornography Is a Left Issue," and we tried to pitch it to *The Nation*. I called up and got one of the editors. I said that we want to talk about pornography and the Left. The first words out his mouth were, "we don't believe in censorship at *The Nation*." I hadn't even mentioned anything about censorship. Then he asked, what about women-owned porn? This is what they always say. I said, let me ask you this: If I were a journalist doing an article on capitalist-controlled media, would the fact that *The Nation* exists disprove everything I'm saying about capitalist-controlled media?

The Left is very masculinized, very patriarchal. I think as long as you have men in power, right or left, women and children are in terrible trouble.

Derrick: I think, in addition, that there's not a Left because the Senate and the House of Representatives are not only proporn but procapitalist. You can't have a Left that's procapitalist, either. The reason I keep hammering this is because, for example, in the United States, if a real anticapitalist Left was a ten on a scale of ten, and a protofascist and procapitalist Right was a one, then basically the United States has a political mainstream between one and three.

Gail: That's exactly right. They've wiped out the left wing in this country. What looks moderate in the U.S. would in Europe be the right wing of the spectrum. In England, for example, we've just had the conservatives voted in, which is awful. But, the conservatives there are the equivalent of the U.S. Democrats. If someone stood up in England and started talking about getting rid of welfare altogether, and getting rid of the health care system, there would be a revolution in the streets. They simply would not tolerate it. England doesn't have a Newt Gingrich, thank god. Nobody like that would survive in mainstream politics.

It's not great, England, but this is what a Left looks like. I remember when I was a kid and there was an election coming up. This was when the Labor Party was really Left, not the "New Labor" of Tony Blair. They asked the treasurer of the Labor Party, "If you get in, what are you going to do?" And this is what he said on national television at six o'clock: "If we get in, I am going to squeeze the rich until they squeak." And, they got in. Can you imagine a politician saying that in America? It would be unthinkable.

Derrick: Given the power of the pornographic—or capitalistic—ideology, how do we get people to engage in a real discussion about the effects?

Gail: It's very difficult because pornography has so colonized the sexual imagination. What we need—and it's one of the reasons we started our group, Stop Porn Culture—is a grassroots organization to start raising consciousness as to the harms of pornography. We put together a slideshow, which has a hundred slides and a fifty-minute script, which we give out free of charge, or it can be downloaded from stoppornculture.org. You can pass it on in your communities, colleges, churches, and homes.

We need to subvert the dominant hegemony of our sexuality. It's very hard, because we don't have access to the mass media. I think the only way to go is to try and treat this as a public health issue, and attack it as we would attack any other public health issue. But, I'll tell you the truth: unless we have a movement, this genie is not going back in the bottle.

The other thing I'm really thinking about seriously is that we, especially the antipornography activists, have an untouched resource out there, which is mothers. Many women are very concerned about their children being brought up in a porn culture, so we need to politicize these women. People always blame parents, and, in a patriarchal culture, when you blame parents, you are really blaming mothers. What can mothers do when they are overwhelmed with just making ends meet? We need to start building a movement based on the power of mothers.

Derrick: How does that apply to wrestling back our culture from corporate predators?

Gail: Ultimately, the planet isn't going to sustain the problems that corporations have caused. We cannot carry on and consume as we are. Throughout the recession economists have talked about growth, as if growth is a good thing. Do they think we can carry on doing this? We need to be talking about how we can have a life once this economic collapse does come. We need to start thinking post-collapse.

Derrick: Just yesterday I was interviewed by Amy Goodman, and one of the things that she asked me about was collapse. I said one of the things that I always say, which is that if you want to see what happens when a patriarchal civil society collapses, look at the Democratic Republic of Congo. Rapes will become even more prevalent and even more organized.

I have two responses to that impending part of the collapse. One, I really like Andrea Dworkin's line, "My prayer for women of the twenty-first century is harden your heart and learn to kill," which in this case means learning self-defense. Two, for men, we need to make our allegiance to the victims of male violence absolute. Real resistance, in this case, means collapse of capitalism, which means chaos, which means probably increased rape, which means we need to prepare for that now. The time to make the allegiance to women absolute is now, not later. That is why a real resistance movement needs a radical feminist analysis.

Gail: I would say the same thing. The Congo, to me, is a perfect example of what happens when masculinity runs amok. That's what men will do if they get license to do it. What's going on in the Congo is intense sexual torture of these women and children.

When we talk about collapse, we're also looking at cultural collapse. The culture cannot sustain this level of pornography. When economic collapse comes, we're going to have men who've been brought up on hardcore pornography running amok. Women are going to have to start figuring out how to protect ourselves and our children. We need to find men of good faith to work with us. There aren't that many, unfortunately.

Derrick: Here's my last question. Why do we have an antiporn activist at an Earth at Risk conference?

Gail: Because cultural sadism is what's fueling all of this. The trouble with patriarchy is not just that men rule it, but that men have this ability to let the worst of men get to the top. That's true, of course, for corporations and pornography, too. Who the hell would ever want to recreate this mess? If anything it tells us that we must have a radical feminist analysis, that we must have women front and center. If you don't have women front and center, you've got a patriarchal, capitalist, racist, imperialist mess.

Do you know what women do really well? We are excellent cleaners. We are excellent at cleaning men's homes, clothes, dishes and underwear. I'm so fucking sick of cleaning up after men. And now we are going to have to clean up the mess they have made of this world. I say to women that we have to stop cleaning up. Enough with cleaning up, already. We need to get some control, and if we don't, then women and children will continue to live in disastrous situations. Men screwed up, and it is now time for them to sit back and give us the chance to create a world worth living in for all of us. That is why we need radical feminism at this conference.

Thomas Linzey

"Under our system of law we treat certain things as property, certain things as persons. Nature is property under our system of law. We've never had an environmental movement because we've never talked about the rights of nature or the rights of ecosystems and what that would look like. We've tried to build an environmental movement based on the concept that if you have a ten-acre piece of property, your deed to that property carries with it the legal right to destroy the ecosystems there."

Derrick Jensen: Thomas Linzey is one of my heroes. He is an attorney and the executive director of the Community Environmental Legal Defense Fund, a nonprofit law firm that has provided free legal services to over five hundred local governments and nonprofit organizations since 1995. He is also cofounder of the Daniel Pennock Democracy School, now taught in twenty-four states across the country, which assists groups in creating community campaigns that elevate the rights of communities over rights claimed by corporations. Linzey is the author of *Be the Change: How to Get What You Want in Your Community.*

Thomas, how did your work as a traditional environmental lawyer transform into helping communities challenge corporate rights and power?

Thomas Linzey: The reason we transformed from doing conventional environmental law to doing something different was because environmental law just wasn't working. And when I say it wasn't working, what I mean is my firm was approached by three-hundred-some community groups between 1995 and 2000. These groups were having difficulties—toxic waste incinerators coming in, natural gas extraction, coal mining—or the thousands of different issues that communities face pretty much every day. These folks would come to us and say, "We don't want this in our community. We want to say 'no' to it. Our idea of sustainable agriculture doesn't include a fifteen-thousand-head hog factory farm smack dab in the middle of the community." And we would patiently explain to them that, well, we would like to say "no" for you as well, but the system of environmental law doesn't allow you to say "no." In fact, the law in the United States today, as it has been for the past hundred years, is that communities are prohibited from banning legal uses. So if a community has a Walmart coming in, and they have a viable downtown that they're trying to preserve, they can't say "no" to Walmart or any other big box stores that want to move there.

Unfortunately, conventional environmental law is all built around that. The fact is, our activism as environmental lawyers basically worked around a system that says people can't actually decide what happens in their own community. We appealed permits and did the regulatory dance and tried to get the corporations to cause a little less harm with whatever project they were trying to develop. Eventually, we took a year or two for soul searching. We shut down our office and said, "We're not going to do this work anymore, because basically we're just helping corporations build better permit applications."

It was about that time that we started getting phone calls from a constituency that we were not set up to assist, which was municipal governments in rural Pennsylvania who were coming to the same conclusion that we were about the status of law. They wanted to work with us to begin drafting local laws themselves that would ban factory farms from coming into central Pennsylvania. Pretty soon those ordinances spread to things like sewage sludge application on lands; folks started banning corporations from doing that in their communities. Eventually, we got to a point where communities were passing laws that stripped corporations of constitutional rights within their municipalities.

So the transformation for us was very quick. We decided to blow out all of our preconceived notions about what environmental law was and what it needed to be. The municipalities with whom we worked began leading the way toward a different kind of law-making. Now it is about seizing municipal governments to turn their lawmaking functions up against the state and federal levels of government, to actually drive sustainability in—because today, sustainability is illegal under our system of law.

Derrick: But if the United States Constitution prohibits sustainability, aren't you wasting your time? Why do you do this if it's all illegal and going to be overturned at the federal level, anyway?

Thomas: That's a great question. I wrote an op-ed called "Illegal and Unconstitutional" because when communities say, "We don't want a factory farm here," the first thing that happens is Hatfield or Smithfield Foods says, "Well, for you to say 'no' to this coming in means you're acting illegally and unconstitutionally." As you know, under our system of law corporations have rights. Corporations have been declared to be persons by the courts, which means they have those full constitutional protections. And under our system of law, as decreed by the U.S. Supreme Court, that means that corporations have more rights than the communities in which they operate, for the most part. So we can accept that status quo or we can begin moving to change it.

The question is, how do we build a movement to dismantle those constitutional provisions and create a new one? We've been working toward that, and we now have 140 communities in the United States that have passed what some people, in the conventional legal community, would call blatantly unconstitutional ordinances. And I think that's the beauty of it. What we're seeing is the first part of a new constitutional revolution in which these communities are blueprinting what a sustainable community looks like at the local level. They're beginning to join hands with other communities across the United States to force that blueprint upward and instigate state constitutional change, and eventually federal constitutional change.

Some people look at the work we do and call it a legal strategy, but it's not really a legal strategy at all. It's an organizing vehicle. Most folks are operating under the illusion that we have a democracy in this country, and if you go into a place and say, "Well, we don't have a democracy in this country," they think you're crazy. And then you say, "Okay, well let's try banning factory farms here. We'll take your hand and walk with you as you do this because you think we have a democracy. We'll help you pass an ordinance banning it." And the next thing that happens in some of these places is that Hatfield or another corporation brings a lawsuit against the community, against the municipality. And they say, "Well, you can't have that law, because we're corporations and we're persons, and what you've done with that ordinance is take our property, which means you've violated our Fifth Amendment rights under the Constitution. In addition to that, you've violated our commerce clause rights, because factory farm production is interstate commerce under the Constitution. In addition to that, there's a rule in the U.S. called Dillon's Rule that says your municipality can't act unless it has been specifically authorized by the state to do so."

The corporation comes in barrels blazing with those doctrines, and pretty soon people realize that what they thought was a factory farm problem is actually a democracy problem. The situation is reframed in the terms of community rights versus corporate rights. And that is why the corporations have started to back off. For example, the City of Pittsburgh passed a hydrofracking ban, which also strips natural gas corporations of constitutional rights within the municipality. Forty-eight hours later, one of the largest gas trade associations in the United States said, "We're not going to sue the City of Pittsburgh." I think they didn't want to sue because, deep down, they understood that it would be a lose-lose for them. Even if they came in and got a court to strike something down, the City of Pittsburgh would go on the offense, because we've set the organizing environment for it.

A lot of folks think the problem is the corporations. But when a corporation wants to move into a community, instead of running into the corporation first—the Walmart, or the Monsanto, or whatever—the community runs into their own constitutional structure of law first, because everything within that constitutional structure of law is privately enforceable by the corporations coming in. The attorney general doesn't sue communities for violating the commerce clause, Walmart does. In addition to that, under our system of law, the corporation can get damages from the municipality—so the corporation can not only overturn the law that the community passed, but punish the elected officials themselves for even daring to pass the law.

Nobody really questions this system or really understands how it works until they've seen it play out in front of them. So our long-term goal here is to assist ten thousand communities across the United States in writing a new system of law that turns the constitutional structure upside down and places the rights of people, communities, and nature above the rights of corporations.

Derrick: You said some things that guarantee you will never be elected president, one of which is that the Constitution is not necessarily the most democratic institution that was ever, well, created by God.

Thomas: Yes. I mean, most Americans think we're the only country with a constitution. There was a poll taken a couple years ago that came to that conclusion. The fact is that the Constitution is a sacred cow within the United States. What's fascinating to me is when people extol the Constitution, they're really not extolling the structural part of the Constitution, the text.

They're extolling the Bill of Rights, which, people forget, had to be forced in by the states and localities because the "founding fathers" didn't want it. And so the Bill of Rights, which we tend to put on a pedestal, was actually driven in by a resistance group of sorts.

The structure of the Constitution is not pretty. In our Democracy Schools, where we train organizers and lawyers and all kinds of folks, we take a look at the Constitution and how it got to us. One

of the things people don't find in most history books is that prior to
the Philadelphia Constitutional Convention, our very own George
Washington, who was one of the largest landowners in the United
States, had a problem. In order to develop his sixty-three thousand
acres of land, he needed to put in canals. Well, Washington was no
slouch; he went to the legislatures of Maryland and Virginia to try
and negotiate a deal to start a corporation that would build the canals. He didn't just go for a charter for the company; he also asked
for a subsidy from Maryland and Virginia.

After ten years, Washington got the charter, but he was so
angry at the legislatures that he came up with a plan and held a
meeting at his place—which we now know as the Mount Vernon
Conference—to discuss the formation of a super-entity that would
actually override the states and localities on issues of commerce.
That turned into the Annapolis Convention, out of which came the
Virginia Plan, which eventually became the U.S. Constitution. So
you see, a big part of the structure of the Constitution was geared
toward finding a way to clothe commerce and property with the
highest protections possible under the constitutional system. Those
protections have extended to the people who own the property and
engage in the commerce. Now, when Walmart wants to move into
town, they have two hundred years of law backing them up. It's like
an iceberg; what we see in the open is not as much as what's under the water. We've accumulated law over the past two hundred
years, and the laws come out of the worst of the worst of this country's history. Corporations use those legal doctrines to control us in
communities.

The question is, how do we dig out from under two hundred
years of bad law, and how long is it going to take? We have a 1790s
plan of governance that was written to guarantee that we could exploit the natural resources, which were seemingly unlimited across
the United States, as quickly as possible. That's what the constitutional structure is about. And goddammit, they did a good job,

because we're still on the receiving end of it now. But it's time to jettison that and build a new constitutional framework.

Derrick: What cultural shift do you see taking place in those communities?

Thomas: It's huge. Many communities are beginning to grapple with this concept that not all property is equal. When they're on the receiving end of a Walmart coming in, they see big property coming in to swallow up their little property. That division between the two, that kind of class warfare happening between people who are relatively privileged and others who are relatively super-privileged, is new to a lot of people. But we're running out of easy to obtain resources, so the corporate boys are coming in to places like Pittsburgh and proposing to drill for natural gas under Catholic cemeteries. When a body dies it pulls oxygen out of every single place it can, even underneath the fingernails. Corporations are pulling in communities that were previously privileged and safe from this kind of exploitation and putting them into a direct line of fire.

We talk a lot about corporations, the "c-word," but these problems are not really about corporations. These problems are caused by a minority of people within the corporate form that have a supersystem of law that privileges them above community majorities. I don't know about you, Derrick, but back in kindergarten I learned that democracy was about something other than that. It wasn't about minorities over majorities, it was actually the opposite way around. And what we have right now is a vested system where the interests are the other way around. People don't see it because since birth we've had it hammered into our heads that the founding fathers were the best folks that ever trod the planet, that the constitutional system is the best system of law ever devised by man. The only folks who are able to come out of that myth-building place and actually begin to engage in a real activism, which is very confrontational and very controversial, are those

who are subject to imminent harm. The fact is, more and more imminent harm is happening in places where it hasn't happened before, and
that's starting to radicalize populations that we wouldn't have thought
would become radicalized prior to this.

Our opponents have helped this along immensely. In
Pennsylvania we had fifty municipalities passing ordinances that
went beyond just stopping imminent harm, but actually decon-
structed the system that enabled the corporation to do what it did in
the first place. The Pennsylvania legislature stepped in, and instead
of stepping in on the side of the communities rather than the corporations, it passed a law authorizing the attorney general of the state
to sue the municipalities to overturn the laws that were passed to
keep the corporations out of those communities. So whereas once
these communities faced off against a Monsanto rep who would
come into the community saying, "Repeal that ordinance or we're
going to sue you," now they faced off against the attorney general
of the state, who said, "If you don't repeal the ordinance that you've
adopted to stop factory farms or whatever else from coming in, we're
going to sue you, not as the corporation, but as the state, using your
taxpayer monies to pay us when we pick up the phone and answer
the call from the Monsanto folks."

When that happened, some people said to us, "Well, that's really
bad for your work, now that the state is shutting it down." But we
thought it was pretty fabulous, because in the beginning people think
that the problem is just the corporation, and it doesn't do any good to
tell them that there's a governmental system behind it that's actually
enabling the corporation to move in. But when the attorney general
stands in a community building and threatens municipal officials and
says, "We're going to sue you in the name of the state," very quickly
the problem is revealed to be this concept of the corporate state. It's a
system problem, not just an errant corporation problem or a corrupt
corporation problem or a greed problem. That framing is so important when people actually move to create a remedy in response.

Derrick: It wasn't until my late twenties or early thirties that I finally realized that laws aren't sacred, and that they're just rules created by rich people to enforce what the rich people want. That's a pretty simple understanding, but it took me years to deconstruct all of my schooling on that subject. I'm not saying that all laws shouldn't exist. I mean, I think it's great that laws against rape exist.

Thomas: Correct.

Derrick: I think the existence of the Clean Water Act is a good thing.

Thomas: Maybe.

Derrick: But that doesn't alter the fact that, by and large, laws are just made up. It's like Eddie Izzard's great skit about the conquest of India.

Thomas: Yes, I've seen that. I love it.

Derrick: In the skit, the British come in and say, "This land is ours." And the people of India say, "Well, you can't do that. We live here." And the British say, "Well, we have a flag." The Indians say, "Well, what difference does that make?" The British answer, "Well, these are the rules that . . . we just made up."

That's basically how conquest works, and it's basically how law works, too. The attorney general says, "Oh, shit, how do we get Walmart into this community that doesn't want it?" Well, "Pass a law, by gum."

Thomas: Absolutely. The British, when they went into India, created a culture of violence that also supported the need for those laws. English common law was used to enable the violence to occur, which was extensive. The British, when they went into India, cut the thumbs off of all the master weavers in India to keep the folks in India dependent upon English textiles. That's the kind of violence that went into colonialism. And that structure of law—that English structure of law—became the U.S. Constitution. They called it the best system of law ever devised on the planet.

Derrick: Which they would, because it served their purposes. I don't think the people of India or Africa or North America would necessarily agree that it's the best system of law.

Thomas: I don't think they would, either. It's like when people say, "The regulatory system is broken. It's not protecting our health, safety, and welfare." And I say, "Well, maybe it's not broken, but it's working perfectly." Because its goal is not necessarily to protect health, safety, and welfare. The law has traditionally been used to shield corporations and allow these things to take place. State agencies don't issue "permits," as they're called, for nothing. They permit something to occur that would otherwise be illegal.

Derrick: I have a great example of that. The frogs in the pond where I live are dying from something called saprolegnia, a mold that attacks weakened egg sacs. The egg sacs are weakened because the weakened ozone layer allows more UVB to come through. So every winter I bring the egg sacs into my house, raise the frogs, and release them. I mentioned this to someone at California Fish and Game.

Thomas: And they said, "Cease and desist."

Derrick: Yes. And this is the same organization that routinely gives permits to clearcutters from Sierra Pacific to raze all the land they want. This woman from California Fish and Game freaked out and said, "You cannot do this. You have to get a permit." And I said, "Great, I'll get a permit. How do I do that?" And she said, "I don't know."

Thomas: We don't have ones for that. Let's invent one.

Derrick: Exactly. It's just crazy.

Thomas: When we practiced traditional environmental law, which was essentially appealing permits and moving through that process, we had several situations where we would catch somebody doing something that they didn't have a permit to do. The state agency would simply retroactively permit the activity. They'd write the permit and send it by fax. It's that kind of stuff that shows what a load of shit this whole system is. It's built on "I say so."

Derrick: I have a legal remedy and a technological remedy to all of our problems that I've been trying to push for quite a while, and since you are an attorney, maybe you could discuss it with me. It's a radio-controlled cigar cutter. The law that I want to get passed would say that before anyone can begin a process for which they need a permit—like if someone wants to put in an oil well in the Gulf of Mexico—all the males associated with the project must guarantee that it's not going to leak oil by having remote-control cigar cutters put on their genitals. If they lie or if the process doesn't work, if the oil well leaks, then *bzzzzt.*

Thomas: I'm with you.

Derrick: It would solve all the problems. Do you think we could get Pittsburgh to pass that?

Thomas: Yes. Maybe we could patent it.

Derrick: And if we were rich, we could actually get a law passed that would enforce this.

Thomas: Absolutely. Or regulate how it's applied and then what current runs through the device.

Derrick: Yes. Okay, let's talk about Pittsburgh. What drove Pittsburgh to become one of the communities you're working with?

Thomas: Hydrofracking for natural gas, which is the new frontier for natural gas extraction. Previously unobtainable assets—gas deposits—are now being opened up by this process, which uses millions of gallons of water to force down boreholes and then blow apart the ground. It is possible to horizontally drill now, so the borehole goes down vertically first, and then it can extend horizontally as much as two miles. Along that path the ground underneath is exploded to obtain the gas from the shale rock. Massive amounts of water are used to break open the shale rock and force the natural gas to the surface.

It's an extremely dangerous, environmentally destructive, aquifer-destroying process. Josh Fox's movie *Gasland* shows folks lighting their faucets on fire from the residue gas that comes out with the water. The water that comes back from this process may also be radioactive. It can't be sent into the treatment plants. Trucks haul it away to western Pennsylvania, and the drivers open up the back of the truck as they're driving and just release the frac water onto the roads.

This is causing a tremendous environmental holocaust. There are ten thousand more well permits being released over the next few years in the state of Pennsylvania, which has become ground zero for this. The City of Pittsburgh had gas leases signed by the gas companies for property that they wanted to drill underneath, including the Catholic cemeteries in the city. City council member Doug Shields, who used to be president of the council, came to us and said, "I want to stop this within the City of Pittsburgh. And we're hoping that if we do it here in the city that other places will do it as well." We worked with him to draft the first local ordinance in the country to prohibit a number of things. It bans natural gas extraction within the city of Pittsburgh. Period. Not just hydrofracking, but all fossil fuel extraction in the city. In addition to that, it strips natural gas corporations of constitutional rights, including commerce clause rights and personhood rights, within the city of Pittsburgh. It also invalidates any state permit issued that contradicts the ordinance. So it carves out a preemption vacuum within the ordinance itself. And perhaps most amazing, it contains a secession clause that says that if any unit of government attempts to preempt this, the city council will be forced to hold meetings to explore forms of separation from the state—from the unit of government that's doing the preempting.

Right now, many people are part of the system that's enabling bad stuff to happen by virtue of nonaction. Silence is assent. But once the system's flaws have been proven to them, these places have begun passing provisions that are a release point, that say, "We now understand what this system's all about. We don't want to be a part of it." The fact that the city of Pittsburgh voted unanimously to adopt an ordinance that deals with an issue like hydrofracking gives me hope in many ways. Another place that gives me hope is Spokane, Washington, which put a community bill of rights on the ballot back in 2009.

Derrick: I lived in Spokane for twelve years. It's conservative as hell.

Thomas: Yes. And in 2009, that bore out. They had a community bill of rights with eleven provisions; it talked about the right to housing, the right to health care, and other rights. It failed by 24 to 76 percent in the city. Then the twenty-four groups that built the bill of rights shortened it slightly and proposed a new community bill of rights with four provisions. One stated that neighborhoods within the city would have the power to say "no" to corporations like Walmart coming in, giving communities veto power against big box stores and other types of development. The second was that the Spokane River actually had legally enforceable rights—in other words, rights of nature. Third, workers would have constitutional rights and rights to collective bargaining within the city. And the fourth provision stated that corporate rights would be subordinated to the rights of the community. This time, the vote was almost 50-50. The proposition didn't get voted in, but it was very close. That's really something in the city of Spokane. It just blew my doors off watching that take place.

Derrick: Tons of money went to the opposition.

Thomas: Yes, last time it was half a million dollars. This time it was a hundred and fifty-some thousand. There were commercials on TV and everything.

Something's happening. It's in the air. For thirty thousand people to cast a vote to give the Spokane River rights, that's pretty amazing stuff, I have to say.

Derrick: Could you talk more about legally enforceable rights, and how environmental law falls short?

Thomas: Environmental law has been a big disaster in many ways. It's all end-of-the-pipe kind of stuff. And we get into fights with environmental lawyers all the time. I have good friends in EDF and NRDC and all the big environmental groups. I now see those groups as impediments to change. They are the ones grabbing on the tightest to regulatory issues and permits and actually giving new life to that kind of system.

When community groups rise up to stop this, that, or the other in their community, there are two calls they make when they pick up the phone. One is to the state, because they think that because a state agency is entitled the Department of Environmental Protection, it actually does something to protect the environment. And the second call they make is usually to an environmental lawyer who's with the Sierra Club or another big environmental group. What's funny is both of those phone calls end up in the same place. The state agency says, "Well, we're very happy that you want to get involved in determining the future of your community, and in this situation it means appealing this permit, which means you have to hire a lawyer and get involved in the permit process." So they run community groups down like cattle in a chute toward the bottom of the regulatory system. The environmental lawyers say—and unfortunately, we did this for six years, too—"Well, you can't stop it. You can't say no to it, but maybe we can help you delay it or make it work a little better, so that it causes a little less harm." They, too, send folks right down the regulatory chute. They all end up at the same place.

Derrick: The slaughterhouse.

Thomas: Yes, where the bolt gets shot through your head. Actually, suicide among farmers is now the number one nonnatural cause of death for farmers in the United States. It's happening in other places, too; in India, people are losing generations-old farms, and they're killing themselves. So we're seeing communities that are concerned about family farmers getting driven out. They are concerned about the environmental and economic impacts this has. They are concerned about the impacts on democracy, too. What happens when four corporations control 80 percent of pork processing in the United States, which is the situation today? They gain political power in the legislatures and then they make more laws, like the ones that we have in Pennsylvania at the attorney general's office. So it doesn't matter what a community's myriad of issues are, or how comprehensive their problem statement is, because eventually they all get channeled to one place where the only topic up for discussion is hog manure, because the state has deemed that the only issue worth addressing is how much liquid manure from factory farms is put on an acre of land.

Let's say you go into court with a factory farm issue unrelated to manure. You try to stand up and talk about the many problems your community is facing. The judge says, "Shut up and sit down. It's not relevant. The only thing that's relevant now is whether that liquid manure is being applied properly." So you have to hire manure experts, and the other side brings in their manure experts, and the judge comes out with a manure decision. But that's all the decision is about. So you see, we're controlled culturally because our activism is not effective. And how stupid are we to think that we can make the regulatory system work when it's written by the very corporations that it's ostensibly supposed to be regulating? Right.

Derrick: You've said that we have not historically had an environmental movement in this country.

Thomas: Yes, I get in trouble for saying that. I said it at Bioneers a number of years ago in the same speech where I quoted you, and I got some feedback from that, too.

Derrick: Speaking of manure.

Thomas: From our vantage point there's never been an environmental movement in this country, because movements are about taking things that were previously treated as property and transforming them into being rights-bearing entities. That's a big mouthful. What does it mean? Well, take the Abolitionists. African Americans were property under the law in the 1850s. There was no such thing as murder of a slave. It was a property damage crime. The perpetrator paid the slave owner with property damages. And up until the 1860s to 1870s, rape was not a crime in the U.S. It was a property damage crime. The perpetrator paid the husband damages. Under our system of law we treat certain things as property, certain things as persons. Nature is property under our system of law. We've never had an environmental movement because we've never talked about the rights of nature or the rights of ecosystems and what that would look like. We've tried to build an environmental movement based on the concept that if you have a ten-acre piece of property, your deed to that property carries with it the legal right to destroy the ecosystems there. It's part of the bundle of rights that comes with property ownership in the Western world.

Derrick: To bring this back to rape, treating women as property also meant historically that if a man owned a wife, he would have rights to sexual access.

Thomas: Yes. And when it comes to nature and ecosystems, that's been the law for ten thousand years.

In 2001, the small borough of Tamaqua, Pennsylvania, in northeastern Pennsylvania—not a particularly progressive place—had dredge coming in from the Delaware River that was laden with PCB. The companies wanted to dump the dredge into old deep mine holes, or boreholes, within the community. The community said, "We don't want that," and they called us. The problem was that nobody owned property near the dump site. Right now under environmental law, the only way you get into court is if you have some kind of property interest that's been interfered with. The residents of this community said, "Well, this doesn't seem right because there are streams there that we fish out of. We use the natural environment, the ecosystems in that area where the dredge is going to be dumped." They wanted to find a different way to protect the environment, and it was in their community that the rights-based approach began. They were the first in the United States to pass a binding local law declaring that nature was not property in their community, but had the right to exist and flourish. For the first time, streams and waterways legally had the right to exist and flourish. People within the community could actually enforce the rights of the river.

Then the folks in Ecuador, who have been used as a cheap hotel for a long time by multinational corporations, heard about what we had done in the United States and brought us down to Ecuador to work with the constitutional drafting committee, several hundred Ecuadorians drafting a new constitution for the country of Ecuador. And they wanted to write rights of nature into their constitution at the national level, and we assisted with that. Their constitution was ratified in 2008, overwhelmingly, by the people in the country of Ecuador, making Ecuador the first country to transform from a property-based system of environmental law to a rights-based system of environmental law. To make the story even more incredible, a few years later the first enforcement action took place. People brought a lawsuit in the name of Ecuador's Vilcabamba River against a local government building a highway that was impacting the river. And they won.

Derrick: What do you mean when you use the term "collective municipal civil disobedience"?

Thomas: Somebody who attended one of our Democracy Schools coined that phrase, because our work is about seizing municipal entities to create the blueprint of law that we've wanted so long to see, and pushing those changes up to the state and federal level.

It is best for civil disobedience to be collective, because when done individually it often ends with police arresting people and saying, "Thank you very much." The criminal enforcement system is then used to put people away or to punish them. So to be effective we need to move and evolve beyond that individual civil disobedience to collective disobedience, just like the four kids who sat-in at the Greensboro Woolworth lunch counter.

Those kids did what they did for two reasons. Number one, because segregation of lunch counters was wrong, and they felt a moral and ethical need to do something about it. But they also did it because they hoped that other people would follow. The next day, more people joined the sit-in. The day after that there were sixty, and the day after there were three hundred. Those numbers aren't exact, but you get the idea. They didn't know so many people would join. One of the kids was interviewed and he said, "Well, I brought my toothbrush, because I knew we were gonna be here a while. You know, getting arrested and being in prison."

I think these municipalities are doing the same thing. These communities are stepping forward and saying, first of all, that the system of law is wrong. They feel a moral need to do something about it. But they also hope that if they do something, maybe somebody else will join. And when somebody else joins, maybe more people will join. Eventually, maybe a critical mass will actually drive changes upward.

Again, it's not just the corporations or the small number of individuals in the corporations causing problems. It's the system that enables corporations to do what they do. That understanding has to be supplanted by a new system of law that actually brings us into the twenty-first century.

Derrick: Your work fits in many places in the resistance culture. One of the things you're doing is building legal alternatives. Is that one way you might categorize your work if you were to choose to do so?

Thomas: I think so. Our work is about tearing down the old bridge while building a new one, and hopefully traffic starts to run across the new one as people experiment with these things. But there is more than one way to dismantle infrastructure. In New Hampshire, for example, there's a big project called Northern Pass where they're trying to wheel energy down from Quebec Hydro to feed the Boston area. People in New Hampshire aren't very happy about it, and they're starting to pass laws that we've drafted. They're going to be on town meeting warrant next year, which goes a step beyond by saying, "We're going to prohibit *all* unsustainable energy systems from running through this community." They're using the power line as a way to begin to define what's sustainable and what's unsustainable, and then applying that to all kinds of other things. Now they're able to say, "We're going to stop that infrastructure from being built before it comes into the community."

I think there are creative ways to use the law that give birth to a variety of different tactics and help people begin to understand what's actually happening to them. I think that understanding is one of the things that has been missing for the past hundred years. The last successful people's movement in this country was the Populist movement at the turn of the century, and they were dismantled pretty quickly. One of the very valuable contributions the Occupy folks have given us is this 99 percent and 1 percent dichotomy. They've given us a way to talk about a corporate class, which is immensely valuable as folks begin to grapple with seizing their own municipalities to make law themselves.

You know, we do a lot of conferences, and I've come to a point where I think that a lot of them are fairly pointless. People come to them for entertainment. It's fun learning about this stuff, and the Democracy Schools are fun, but we're looking for the people who are actually going to get shit done. Ten years ago, we'd go to a conference and speak to a thousand people, and there would be applause, and everybody would be happy—but there would be very few people coming forward to say, "I want to do that where I live." Now we don't go to any events except those that are calculated to lead to finding individual people who are actually going to do the work. We've transformed ourselves from trying to galvanize public education to finding those individual people who for some reason or the other are as crazy as you and I to actually think that they can do something to disrupt the entire system, to throw everything back against the folks that are doing us harm. Those people are very precious to us. They tend to be self-confident, and a lot of them are kids. We had somebody come three thousand miles to work on the Envision Spokane campaign, and that person is now a staff member of ours working in Pennsylvania. We give jobs to people who help us run these community campaigns so that people can earn a living doing this work. One of the big challenges we have now is finding out how to construct a new system with enough resources to bring more people in.

Waziyatawin

"This is a system, this wonderful creation that needs all of us, including human beings. We are part of it, even though this culture has worked to systematically destroy those good relations and those ecosystems."

Derrick Jensen: Waziyatawin is a Dakota writer, teacher, and activist committed to the development of liberation strategies that will support the recovery of Indigenous ways of being, the reclamation of Indigenous homelands, and the eradication of colonial institutions.

I think it's crucial that, when it comes to anything concerning sustainability or resistance, Indigenous Peoples must have the final say.

Waziyatawin: The problem that we've been facing for 518 years is that every city in the Western Hemisphere has been built on the lands and over the bodies of Indigenous people. They continue to suffer and the land continues to suffer so that cities can be here, so that this university can be here, and so that we can be here today. We should never, ever forget that.

Derrick: How do we begin to talk about the process of colonization?

Waziyatawin: It's important that we think about colonization as a process, and conquest as a component of that process, but it begins with invasion. Certainly, in the Western Hemisphere, we have experienced what I think is the most brutal period of colonization in world history, and it has lasted for more than five centuries. I think we are coming to the end of that period, so in some ways I'm filled with a sense of hope, and in some ways I'm filled with a sense of absolute rage.

Derrick: Tell me more about the processes of colonization. What are its effects on the self-image and social image of conquered people? Also, could you tie that together with what Vine Deloria Jr. said about how this is a crucial time, because the last people who talked to people who were born free are now dying?

Waziyatawin: In my life, I've never known freedom. I've never known liberation. I've only dreamt of it a million times; I've imagined it. I've never experienced it. In fact, the elders with whom I grew up also never experienced it directly, because they had all died long before I was born. The process of colonization has obviously had a devastating effect on the land, but it also has a devastating effect on the capacity for Indigenous Peoples to live our role as defenders of the land.

One of the women who fought fearlessly and courageously in Canada was named Harriet Nahanee. She was also a residential school survivor. She has one of the best quotes about the colonization of the mind, one that occurred to her during her residential school experience. She said, "We were keepers of the land. That is the special job given to our people by the creator. And the whites wanted the land, the trees, and the fish, so they had to brainwash us to forget we had to guard and preserve the land for the creator. That's why they put us in the residential schools and terrorized us: so we'd forget our language, and our laws, and allow the land to be stolen. And it worked; the whites have 99 percent of the land now, and our people are dying off. That's why it's never been about God or 'civilizing' us. It's always been about the land."

When I think about what has happened in the Dakota context—that's what I can speak about with the most authority— it's clear that according to our conceptions of the world, we were Indigenous in the most fundamental sense. One of the reasons that I always prefer the term "Indigenous" is because of its connotations of coming from the land, emerging from the land. According to the

Bdewakantunwan Dakota creation story, which is a story that I grew up with, the place of Dakota creation occurs at a place we call *Bdote*, which literally means the joining or junction of two bodies of water. In a place like Minnesota, the place where I come from and where we have almost fifteen thousand rivers and streams and another six thousand lakes, there are a lot of places that we could refer to as that junction. But, I was always taught that the primary junction is the place where the Minnesota River joins the Mississippi River. It's filled with silt and topsoil. According to this story, our Mother Earth opened up her body and our people were created from red clay from that location. We are Indigenous in the most fundamental sense, and we were taught that our way of life and everything about who we are is central to that landbase. It doesn't make sense to be Dakota in any other place, because that's where our people were created. Our language, our ceremonies, our sacred sites, our worldview are all connected to that particular place. It's no wonder that when we faced invasion, land theft, and colonization, our people eventually went to war. Our major war occurred in 1862 when our people declared war against not just the United States government as an entity, but its citizens, because they were the face of the United States government and the ones who were actually invading our lands.

Colonization of the mind, which has been conducted very successfully in the context of the United States and Canada, is really about disconnecting us from our landbase, disconnecting us from our responsibility to defend the land, even though I would say that is our very first obligation as Indigenous people. We have, in many ways, succumbed to settler society's ideas about what a proper relationship with the land is, and that's about exploitation. So, we have people within our own communities—our tribal leaders, our own band council leaders—who are now essentially selling our landbase for exploitation. We've become complicit. We've become complacent, as a whole.

I want to qualify that by also saying that we also have Indigenous people who haven't forgotten that fundamental obligation, and who continue to fight and challenge power on a daily basis in defense of the land, in defense of our people, in defense of our ways of life.

Derrick: What do you see as the root problem of the dominant culture? And—this is a question I think a lot of Indigenous people have asked for the last 518 years—why do they act the way they do?

Waziyatawin: That's a really important question. When I think about the context of the Western Hemisphere, and the devastation brought to the lands here, I think it's really important for all of us to understand that Judeo-Christian thought is at the center. There is a quote from Genesis 1:26 that states that God said, "Let us make men in our image, in our likeness, and let them rule over the fish of the sea and the birds of the air, over the livestock, over all of the earth, and over all of the creatures that move along the ground."

It's such a captivating section, I think, because it's so visually clear. It's about domination. It's about the subjugation of all beings and about man being at the pinnacle of this hierarchy of creation. I think that concept, that idea, is so pervasive and deeply embedded in this society; so deeply embedded that it is the cultural paradigm by which the United States government operates and this whole society operates. I don't think Christianity is salvageable in any way. I don't think the United States government is salvageable; I'm not interested in preserving American democracy.

From my perspective, this culture and its people have absolutely forfeited their right to participate in envisioning what a different world should look like. That's why I think Indigenous alternatives have to be explored. Indigenous Peoples' relationships with the land have to be given primacy. One of the things that is rarely mentioned when people talk about creating alternative communities—or even when they invoke the rhetoric of utopian societies—is that Thomas

More's society displaced Indigenous populations, moved Indigenous populations out of the way. We can't forget that. As soon as we start to imagine a future based on that kind of model, we're running into the same problems. We're assuming that the original people of the land are expendable, don't have something to teach, and I think that is a very grave mistake.

When I think about indigeneity, I think about what is at the core of our spirituality. It's the idea of Mother Earth and kinship with creation. In Dakota tradition, we have a phrase that I think has been largely co-opted or appropriated by many circles: *mitakuye owas'in,* or "all my relations." People sometimes use it as a quaint phrase today, or invoke it when they want it to serve their political, personal, or spiritual agendas, but in fact it goes much deeper than that in our traditions. That phrase refers to our spiritual obligation to establish good relations with all of creation.

Embedded in that phrase are a couple of assumptions. One is that all beings have a particular role and particular purpose in the world, and we have an obligation to respect that, even though we may not have yet discovered what that role is. We have to assume they have their own gifts and something they are bringing to the world that is necessary.

The other assumption with that is that there is recognition of the fundamental interconnectedness of all of creation. I think this is something that Western societies are only starting to comprehend now; that when one population is affected, all populations are affected. This is a system, this wonderful creation that needs all of us, including human beings. We are part of it, even though this culture has worked to systematically destroy those good relations and those ecosystems. From a Dakota perspective—and I would think that most Indigenous populations would share this—we are part of that, we aren't separate from nature or the land. We are, in fact, the land. We are also needed. As Indigenous populations, I think we've fulfilled those roles in oftentimes ceremonial or spiritual ways, where we understand that things operate in a particular landbase in a particular way, and that it's our obligation to perform certain ceremonies or sing to the salmon or sing to the buffalo. It's one of the reasons why I think that no alternative community or future can be created on this landbase without consulting and working with Indigenous populations, who are just as important to the land as other species.

Derrick: When you say that no future can be created without consulting, some problems come up. The first is that the dominant culture has a long history of consulting before taking. Also, who is doing the consulting?

Waziyatawin: I'm referring to giving primacy to Indigenous populations in their determining what should happen on any given landbase.

Derrick: Given that and given the fact that those in power have tanks, guns, airplanes, and the full force of the law behind them, as well as a mass of zombies who watch television a lot, what does this mean for Indigenous sovereignty or the future of the land?

Waziyatawin: My sense of hope comes from my belief that everything is in place for collapse to occur soon. I think we're seeing the failure of capitalism and, as William Catton pointed out, we are in overshoot. We are running out of fossil fuels to exploit, and this can't go on much longer. Unlike my ancestors, who fought a war of resistance in defense of the land, our people, and our way of life in 1862, we're now positioned for a kind of success that is unprecedented. I am a historian by training, but I think in many ways we cannot look to historical examples to be our models for what is going to happen. We exist in a particular point in world history and human history that is absolutely unique. Everything about this way of life is utterly dependent on cheap fossil fuels. When that is taken away, this is all going to collapse. This way of life as we know it will not exist anymore.

We're in a different place with different opportunities available to us, and if we measure success by the collapse of industrial civilization, I absolutely believe that we will be successful.

Derrick: It reminds me of something I wrote in *What We Leave Behind*. We were fighting a developer—a killer, a person who was going to put a bunch of houses into a forest—and we in the neighborhood fought knowing that all we could do was make sure that everything was perfect in his permits. We ended up stopping him from putting houses in because we were able to delay him long enough for the economic collapse to hit. This wasn't actually our strategy; our strategy was just to hold him off as long as possible. A few months ago his house was foreclosed for back taxes and the main forester's house was foreclosed for bankruptcy, which is great.

We are speaking positively about the collapse of industrial civilization. I was recently in a public forum where I was accused of being unethical for simply saying that this way of life is unsustainable. What do you say when someone critiques you for looking forward with anticipation to the end of civilization?

Waziyatawin: This is one of the few times when I think being an Indigenous person might be an advantage, because people have a hard time saying that to me with a straight face. Indigenous populations suffered an extermination rate of 98.5 percent in the Western Hemisphere.

Derrick: So, we shouldn't use past tense.

Waziyatawin: Absolutely. We're still suffering.

Indigenous populations are no doubt recovering, but we're also still under assault in what can only be called ongoing genocidal campaigns to either directly attack our bodies physically—especially Indigenous women—or through ongoing assaults to our lands and way of life, which continue to affect our capacity to feed ourselves in the most basic sense.

The question you are asking me is, how do I morally respond to the idea that there will be millions of deaths as a consequence of collapse?

Derrick: Yes. Part of my answer is, what people are we talking about? Is it the salmon people, the hammerhead shark people, the coral people, the bison people? Indigenous languages are disappearing at a relatively quicker rate than Indigenous nonhumans. The arguments don't really hold there.

Another answer is that years ago I asked Anuradha Mittal, former director of Food First, if the people of India would be better off if the global economy disappeared tomorrow. She laughed and said of course, because there are former granaries of India that now export dog food and tulips to Europe.

The question for me becomes, which people are dying? That doesn't alter the fact that a lot of people are going to die.

Waziyatawin: I feel like the question misses the point. It's irrelevant, because it doesn't matter what I think. If I could dictate how the world should be, I would be making all kinds of changes. But, I didn't personally create the situation that we're in, so to talk about how dire the situation is, is not a responsibility or sense of guilt that I take on.

Derrick: So, to say it's unethical to say that that a lot of people are going to die in the crash is like saying that if you jump off a cliff, you're going to die?

Waziyatawin: Exactly.

Derrick: One argument made in support of industrial civilization continuing is that we can't go "backward," and that nobody wants to live in caves or mud huts or any of the insulting clichés. I'm sure you get this all the time.

Waziyatawin: I love this question, when people ask it of me, because I think it reveals one of the dominant paradigms of this society, which is an investment or subscription to the notion of linear time. Vine Deloria wrote extensively on the relationships between science and religion and Indigenous populations, particularly Indigenous cosmologies. He wrote about linear time as being something deeply embedded in Judeo-Christian thought. In the Bible, it's the way time is described and the way our relationship with the world is described. It starts with the origin, an act of creation by god, and presumably ends with the coming of Jesus Christ. There is a beginning and an end. Even science, which has broken off from religion and become what is supposed to be a secular tradition, it's still using that same paradigm, still searching for the origins.

In Dakota, there is not a direct translation of linear time, and I suspect it's the same in many Indigenous societies, because we didn't subscribe to a notion of linear time. There are thousands of cultures around the world who don't see time in a linear way, but instead see things in cycles, in ages, in transformation between birth and death, and those cycles repeat themselves, but there is no beginning or end. When people ask a question about something being "backward," then there has to be something that is "forward," and you start to see it's deeply intertwined with this notion of "progress."

Indigenous populations were always backward, according to this framework, because it is believed that there was a natural progression from savagery to civilization, and that all peoples eventually traverse that trajectory. In effect, that's not true; if Dakota people were left in our homelands for the next ten thousand years, I would expect that our people would look very similar to the way they did prior to invasion. Again, it's about a different set of core values. Rather than being invested in the idea of "progress" or some kind of advancement, the fundamental values are instead rooted in concepts of balance and reciprocity, establishing good relationships, upholding what is sustainable in the long term. That's why there are Indigenous populations around the world who can live on the same landbase for thousands of years. They understand these core principles.

When you expose that reliance on a concept like linear time, then the paradigm flips. If you start to examine societies from a different lens, you see the wisdom of having a life based on balance, reciprocity, and sustainability, versus the folly or idiocy of continuing to work toward a notion of progress that is based on the ruthless exploitation of finite sources and in destroying the land upon which you need to live.

Derrick: What has been your process of decolonization?

Waziyatawin: Like all Indigenous Peoples today in North America, decolonization for me has been, at times, a very painful process, because all of us have now been indoctrinated in the same kinds of values and beliefs as settler society. If we were fortunate enough to be raised in a family or community where there is an alternative narrative, then we approach colonizer values and ideas with a critical perspective. Or, if we've experienced some kind of critical intervention along the way that causes us to question our adherence to settler ideas and values, then we're better positioned to work on our own decolonization.

For me, it feels like it's been a very slow process. I was fortunate enough to be raised in a family with alternative ideas about things, but I clearly was influenced by other ideas as well. One example is my work in truth-telling. I'm a professional educator, and one of the reasons I went into the field of history and teaching was because I believed that if people just understood the truth about what happened, that they would change. That's really hard to let go of, because what I've learned from firsthand experience in efforts of truth-telling is that people really don't care, for one. They care about power and privilege. They care about investing in a particular way of life, and the truth is irrelevant to that. The older I get and the more experiences like that I have, the more I've come to believe that there isn't any way you can work within the existing system to radically change it. It's flawed at the core. That's what I mean when I say it's not salvageable. It all needs to come down. All of it.

Derrick: How would you define decolonization for a white person? What do you as an Indigenous person want from white allies?

Waziyatawin: When I talk about decolonization or the process of colonization and how that's carried out with different populations, the logical pathway to decolonization involves the colonizers leaving, going back, ending their colonization of other people's lands. This is something that was advocated in other parts of the world when Indigenous populations engaged in decolonization movements. I think we're in a different situation here, in the United States and Canada, largely because Indigenous populations still are so small in comparison with the rest of the population. Given the extermination rates of our people already, I have no doubt that if we advocated that, then a more aggressive campaign of extermination would be waged against us. What I believe is that we're going to have to work something out.

When I talk about decolonization today, I talk about overturning all of the systems and institutions of colonialism. That means everything in American society and this way of life. It means the economic system, the governmental system, the education system, the criminal injustice system, everything. All aspects of it need to get taken down; that's what decolonization looks like.

I think in an academic context, especially when we're talking about the Western Hemisphere, people get funny ideas about what decolonization is; they think that it's about tweaking the existing system or reform. When I use the term decolonization, I mean all of it has to go. If people are interested in being allies in a struggle for decolonization—which is closely aligned with the need to take down industrial civilization—then it means they need to take seriously the responsibility to help bring about the collapse of all these systems and institutions.

As an Indigenous person, I am advocating for the development of a resistance movement for Dakota people in Dakota homeland. That's what this shirt I'm wearing is about; it says "Defend *Minisota*." *Minisota* is our ancient name for our homeland: *Minisota Makoce*, which might translate as "land where the waters reflect the skies." It's a geographically specific term. When I'm talking about defending *Minisota*, I'm talking about Dakota people rising up and defending our land, because it's currently being destroyed. One of the realities we face as Dakota people is that Minnesota's and the U.S. policies of genocide and ethnic cleansing were so extraordinarily successful that many of our people live in exile today. Our people who do live in *Minisota* are confined to such small pieces of land. We have a total of about five or six thousand acres, which is about 0.012 percent of our original landbase. If we had to rely on our landbase today for survival, we would starve within a matter of days. What does it mean when we live in a society that continues to disallow our people to return from exile—to return home—and to live as original people on our landbase?

This resistance struggle is originating among Dakota people in our homelands, and I think we do have some allies who will join this struggle and fight with us. I also believe in the need for Indigenous populations to resume their roles as defenders of the land, but in some ways this is very scary, because while Indigenous populations have and continue to put their lives on the line in defense of the land, most people who have benefited most from our dispossession still take no action. My biggest fear in advocating that

Indigenous Peoples resume that role in a very serious and committed way is that largely white allies who know what needs to happen, but who are too cowardly to take action, will allow us to take the bullets again.

Derrick: What do you think is necessary for Indigenous Peoples to revive, develop, or engage in strategies of resistance?

Waziyatawin: A couple of things. First, I want to say that decolonization for Indigenous populations has two major components. One is resurgence, and the other is resistance. When I talk about resurgence, it means putting faith, once again, in the traditions, values, belief systems, stories, and prophecies that have sustained our people for thousands of years. There was wisdom in those. Settler society has tried to make us forget that wisdom, and we need to embrace it once again. Resurgence is about recovering those ways of being, those ways of thinking, those ways of praying.

The other component is resistance.

Derrick: Which, as we've talked about, can be as straightforward as learning to tan a hide.

Waziyatawin: Absolutely, we'll need all of those skills. When we talk about resistance, there are a few quotes that I want to bring up.

The first is a quote from Tecumseh, who was a Shawnee leader of resistance in the early nineteenth century. At one point, he was trying to rally support from other Indigenous populations to create a united resistance effort. His speeches are amazing. Here is one quote from him: "Will we let ourselves be destroyed in our turn without a struggle; give up our homes, our country, given to us by the Great Spirit, the graves of our dead, and everything that is dear to us? I know you will cry with me: never, never." It's that cry that we need to revive among our people again.

But there's also another kind of effort that needs to be taken up today, because we're in a unique historical time period. We're facing a unique situation. I want to bring up a quote by Lee Maracle, who is a Stó:lō Indigenous intellectual in Canada. She says, "To win, we must plan in the cellars and attics, lurking in the dark with one eye cast about for the enemy. In our heart of hearts, we know the enemy is a beast that will stop at nothing to keep his world intact. We know that his money comes to him dripping from every pore with the blood and toil of millions. We know the enemy is ever-watchful, on guard day and night against the potential threat we all pose. To plan, we must learn to sum up our history; not the history of betrayal, but the history of our resistance. We must learn from our mistakes, and chart the course for our eventual victory." What I love most about this particular quote is that she's talking about a strategy that Indigenous people here haven't taken up in quite that way. She's also talking about our resistance fighters, and we've realized that in the context of defending *Minisota*, that is precisely what we've been doing; we've been going back to the historical records. I've already written about the crimes against humanity perpetrated against Dakota people: the genocide, the ethnic cleansing, the bounties, the land theft, the dispossession, and the concentration camps. We know those things and have talked about them. Now it's time to invoke that spirit of resistance.

There are some lessons from our historical experience that we can now bring forward and work with. One of the lessons that we learned from our war in 1862—which we lost, obviously, in a matter of about five and a half weeks—is that it made no difference whether someone was considered a hostile to the United States government and its citizens, or whether one was considered a friendly. In the end, we were all subjected to the same treatment: we all lost our homeland, we were all colonized. If we know that today, then the lesson is that we should all be fighting, because you aren't going to curry favor within this society by going along. You're only going to help defeat the resistance.

Derrick: One of the main German resisters in World War II was the mayor of Leipzig, I believe, who was a stout pacifist, but nonetheless believed that Hitler was terrible. He believed that he could just talk to Hitler and that he would be able to talk him out of policies. When the whole final coup attempt failed, he was tortured and killed along with everyone else, even though he was an absolute pacifist who refused to go along with any plan that was possibly violent.

Waziyatawin: You may as well take up arms.

If my Dakota ancestors would have been able to see the devastation that would occur within our homeland—if they could have seen a vision of what our homeland looks like today and know what this society would do to our beloved homeland—they would have fought a lot harder. Certainly, in 1862, we had people who betrayed our resistance fighters, and we paid a price because of that. Now, today, I think that we all know that this culture is not going to give up this way of life voluntarily. It's not going to happen through persuasion. Knowing that and knowing the trajectory we're on, we need to stop that trajectory by any means necessary and be serious and strategic about it. The longer this culture is allowed to continue on this trajectory, the worse it will be. It's in everyone's best interest to act as quickly as possible. We need to prepare and get ourselves trained. If we don't have skills, we need to develop them. But, we can all start with smaller actions right away.

The other thing that makes our situation today unique is that we're going to have major windows of opportunity, because the system, the culture, is already collapsing—it's teetering. The economy, as you pointed out, is one weak area. Infrastructure and other things reliant on cheap oil are going to provide windows of opportunity where our actions can have the most impact. We need to prepare for big actions when those windows of opportunity arise.

Today, I talk often with young people. I have three children—one is twenty, and two are teenage boys—who are all aware that we're going to be engaged in a serious struggle. When I talk to them, my be-loved children, what kinds of things do I tell them? I tell them that we need to stop symbolic actions. I've engaged in my share of symbolic actions. Even now, today, things will come up in Dakota territory and I think to myself: I can't be silent about this. I'm here, and it hurts me to be quiet. It's difficult to not want to engage in some kind of sym-bolic action. But, it's not going to do any good, I'm firmly convinced.

If you're going to invest in resistance, take action underground. Don't talk to another person about what you're doing, unless it's the people you're going to be taking the actions with. I've made the mis-take of being very public about what I'm advocating, which means that I'll be one of the first people caught. Don't get caught; prevent yourself from getting caught as long as possible.

When I think about the work I'm doing, I think about indigene-ity as people and lands and plants and animals and waters. They are the audience to whom I direct most of my work and energy, because they are who I'm committed to. For Indigenous populations, we re-ally need to revive that spirit of resistance.

One quote that has taken on additional meaning to us as Dakota people in thinking about reviving a resistance movement comes from Little Crow, who was our leader of resistance in 1862. The quote is in English, although he originally would have spoken this in Dakota. It's going to sound a little more awkward here because I'm going to change the pronouns a little bit. In Dakota, when we use pronouns, they can be male or female; they aren't gender-specific. Even when we use the word that can be translated as "man," it can also be trans-lated as "people."

These are words that Little Crow spoke in 1862. He said, "I tell you, we must fight and perish together. A man is a fool and coward who thinks otherwise and who will desert his nation at such a time. Disgrace not yourselves to those who will hang you up like dogs, but die, if die you must, with arms in your hands, like warriors and braves of the Dakota."

When I think about that, and when I think about the struggle that we all face, I know it is time for everyone to come forward and be willing to risk something. Eventually, even people engaged in permaculture, if they are feeding a resistance movement, are going to be targeted for persecution. They are going to risk torture, imprisonment, and death. We are all going to have to risk something, so get over it. This is a long-term struggle, and you have to be thinking beyond yourself. You have to be thinking about future generations and animals and plants. It is way beyond you as an individual, so get over it and engage in struggle.

Derrick: You have a shirt—and you also gave me a shirt—that says "Fuck Patience." Can you briefly talk about fucking patience?

Waziyatawin: That comes from a conversation among Indigenous people. One of the favorite quotes that I have of yours is the "too kind" quote. Vine Deloria Jr. used to talk about something similar as well. He talked about Indigenous Peoples being too polite, saying that we have been afraid of "offending" others. I had a conversation among an Indigenous group of people, and one of the elders talked about the need for having patience. He said we need to have patience with little brother, with white people, who are screwing things up because of immaturity, because they are still babies, really. We need to help bring them along.

It was in that context that I thought: we don't have time. I feel the urgency way too strongly. We don't have time for this society, for this culture to come to its senses. We need to take action and we need to do it now. I thought of this message: "Fuck Patience."

Lierre Keith

"The ruling religion of this planet is called patriarchy. We will not save life on earth until we dismantle masculinity."

Derrick Jensen: Lierre Keith is a writer and radical feminist activist. She's the author of two novels as well as *The Vegetarian Myth: Food, Justice, and Sustainability*, which has been called the most important ecological book of this generation. She is coauthor of *Deep Green Resistance: Strategy to Save the Planet*.

Lierre, what is the problem with civilization?

Lierre Keith: Civilization depends on agriculture. So first, you have to understand what agriculture is. In very brute terms, you take a piece of land, you clear every living thing off it, and I mean down to the bacteria, and then you plant it to human use. So agriculture is biotic cleansing.

There are two problems with this. The first one is that it lets the human population grow to really big numbers, because instead of sharing that land with millions of other creatures, you're only growing humans on it. The second problem is that it destroys the soil. And soil is the basis of life; well, land life anyway. We owe our entire existence to six inches of soil and the fact that it rains. So except for the last forty-six remaining tribes of hunter-gatherers, the human race has now made itself dependent on an activity that is destroying the planet. This is not a plan with a future. It's drawdown. And what's being drawn down is fossil soil, fossil water, and species. Entire ecosystems are being drawn down. But the soil is the point here.

In one season of planting a basic row crop—rice or corn or wheat—you can run through two thousand years of soil. On the first day of the Dust Bowl, there were farms that lost *all* of their topsoil in one day. So this is drawdown in a huge way. Think of Iraq—this is the very first place that agriculture started. I don't think anyone in their right mind could call it the Fertile Crescent anymore. Or think of Iran: 94 percent of the land has been degraded. Or China: the dust storms from China are so bad now that they are creating asthma in children in Denver, Colorado. The dust comes across the Pacific, hits the mountains, and comes down. That's how much dust.

Again, when you destroy soil, you're destroying the basis of life. And Jared Diamond, who won a Pulitzer Prize, said that agriculture was the biggest mistake the human race has ever made. Toby Hemenway calls sustainable agriculture an oxymoron, and Richard Manning uses exactly the same sentence. Manning is worth quoting. He writes, "No biologist, or anyone else for that matter, could design a system of regulations that would make agriculture sustainable. Sustainable agriculture is an oxymoron. It mostly relies on an unnatural system of annual grasses grown in a monoculture, a system that nature does not sustain or even recognize as a natural system. We sustain it with plows, petrochemicals, fences, and subsidies, because there is no other way to sustain it."

Burn those four sentences into your brain.

Agriculture is the most destructive thing that people have done to the planet. I'm going to repeat that: agriculture is the single most destructive human activity.

Remember what agriculture is. You pull down the forest, you plow up the prairie, you drain the wetland, you destroy the living communities that our planet would naturally create. And what used to be habitat for millions of creatures, doing that basic work of life, turns into salt and dust. Agriculture is carnivorous; it eats entire ecosystems. And that is what it has done around the globe.

To state the obvious, no culture that is destroying the basis of life itself can be called sustainable. Really, it can only be called insane.

Agriculture has run through every continent. Well, all of them except Antarctica. But that's okay, we'll get that one with global warming. Actually, agriculture marks the beginning of global warming. It's also the beginning of militarism, and it depends upon slavery. In the seven centers where agriculture began, human societies follow the same pattern, and it's called civilization. To use a really basic definition, that just means "life in cities." But when I say civilization, it is not a good thing. It's people living in settlements big enough that they require the importation of resources. They have used up what the land upon which they live can give them. They need more. So they have to go out and get whatever it is they need—food, water, energy—because they've used up their own. By definition, they have overshot their landbase. This is the pattern of civilization everywhere. There's a bloated power center surrounded by conquered colonies, from which the power center takes what it wants.

Agricultural societies end up militarized—and they always do—for three reasons. The first is that agriculture creates a surplus, and if it can be stored, it can be stolen. Somebody has to guard it. Those people are called soldiers.

The second problem is imperialism. Agriculture is essentially a war against the natural world. It's inherently destructive, and eventually the agriculturalists use up what they have—their soil, their trees, and their water. They've got to go out and get those from somewhere else, but people do not willingly give up their land, their water, their trees. Since the power center needs those things, there's an entire class of people whose job is to go out and get them. Agriculture makes that possible. It also makes it inevitable.

Problem number three, of course, is slavery. Agriculture is back-breaking labor. For anyone in an agricultural society to have leisure, there need to be slaves. We've lost the cultural memory of this because we've been using fossil fuel to do that labor for the last hundred and fifty years. But by the year 1800, fully three-quarters of people on the planet were in some form of indenture, slavery, or serfdom. Three-quarters. That's how much labor it takes to do this. The only reason we've forgotten that is because we're using machines now. But I guarantee you, when the fossil fuel runs out, we're going to remember exactly how much labor is involved.

Once huge numbers of the population are in slavery, someone has to keep them there, and that would be the soldiers. This is a cycle we've been in for ten thousand years.

Here is why the agriculturalists will always win, at least in the short term. It takes six hundred old growth trees to make a tall ship. If you are willing to destroy your forests, you're going to win against the people who aren't willing to destroy theirs. Eventually you're going to have to conquer the people who aren't willing to destroy their trees, so you can take them. That's the last ten thousand years in two sentences.

By the year 1950, this planet was out of topsoil. What happened next was the Green Revolution, and that was based on fossil fuel. At this point, if you're eating grain, you're eating oil on a stalk. You're not just eating fossil soil, you're eating fossil fuel. It takes somewhere in the neighborhood of three to four tons of TNT per acre to keep the average American farm running. Iowa alone uses the energy equivalent of four thousand Nagasaki bombs every year. That's how much energy goes into this.

The very creation myth of Western civilization tells men to dominate, to conquer, to go forth and multiply. No hunter-gatherer is told by god to willfully overshoot the landbase, and no marginally rational person would listen to such a god. But that is what we are up against. This is a culture of profound entitlement, based on a masculine violation imperative. That imperative includes violating the sexual boundaries of women and children; the biological boundaries of rivers and forests; the genetic boundaries of other species; and ultimately, the physical boundaries of the atom itself.

The ruling religion of this planet is called patriarchy. We will not save life on earth until we dismantle masculinity. You will be punished for saying that out loud. But we have got to gather up our courage and do it anyway, because our planet really is at stake.

Derrick: When you talk about the masculine "imperative to violate," you're not talking about biology.

Lierre: No, patriarchy takes a group of people who are biologically male and turns them into a social class of people called "men." Masculinity has nothing to do with biologically what you are or aren't. This is a political arrangement. It's not natural, it was not created by god. It's a corrupt and brutal arrangement of power.

Derrick: So what do we need?

Lierre: Well, if this is a war, we need a resistance movement. One of my favorite people from history is Christabel Pankhurst, the strategic genius behind the British Suffragist movement who said, "We know that relying solely on argument, we wandered for forty years politically in the wilderness. We know that arguments are not enough and that political force is necessary." My other favorite is Frederick Douglass, who said, "Power concedes nothing without a demand. It never did and it never will." Again, if this is a war, we need a resistance movement. Ask yourself this question: do you think this war is a metaphor, or is it real?

Now, there are a substantial number of people on the Left who would say, well, not only is this war a metaphor, but I'm using the wrong metaphor. There's no enemy, there's no us and them, there are only well-meaning, if wounded, people.

That cuts right to the main division between liberals and radicals. The liberals believe that society is made up of individuals. In this view, individualism is so sacrosanct that being identified as a member of a group or class is insulting. On the radical side, it's totally different. And we owe this debt to Karl Marx, whether we're Marxist or not. He's the one who figured out that society is not made up of individuals, it's made up of classes of people. His insight was about economic class, but this includes any group or caste. And some of those groups have power over other groups. So this is not an individual condition. Being a member of a group is not any kind of an affront. Far from it. Identifying with a group of people is the first step toward political consciousness, and ultimately, effective action. You make common cause with the people who share your condition.

The other big division is in the nature of social reality. Liberalism is idealist. In this view, social reality is made up of ideas, of attitudes, and therefore social change happens through rational argument and education.

But on the radical side, society is organized by concrete systems of power. Not thoughts and ideas, but material conditions, material institutions. So for radicals, the solution to oppression is to take those systems apart brick by brick. The liberals say we have to educate, educate, educate, and the radicals say, "No, actually we have to stop them." When power is removed from the equation—as it is in the liberal view—oppression looks voluntary, which erases the fact that it's social subordination. I think often of Harriet Tubman, who said, "I've freed hundreds of slaves and I could have freed hundreds more, if they had but known they were slaves." That is a very poignant way to say the same thing.

People withstand oppression using three psychological methods: denial, accommodation, and consent. Anyone on the receiving end of domination learns early in life to stay in line or risk the consequences. And those consequences only have to be applied once in a while to be effective. From that point forward, the traumatized psyche will police itself. So, *if they had but known they were slaves.*

Any show of resistance is met with a continuum that starts with derision, and ends with out and out violence.

But resistance does happen somehow. Once some understanding of oppression is gained, most people are called to action. And I think that's our hardest job as radicals: breaking through that denial, accommodation, and consent.

There are four broad categories of response to injustice: legal remedies, direct action, withdrawal, and spirituality. These categories can overlap in ways that are crucial to resistance movements; all of them can also be diversions that dead-end. None of them are definitively liberal or radical in themselves. If you walk away with nothing else from this, that's what I want you to remember. All four of these categories have key strengths for resistance movements, but we have to understand them strategically.

Before I describe the four responses to injustice, I want to reiterate this: social change requires force. Why? Because it's not a mistake out of which the powerful can be educated.

Don't misunderstand me, please. When I say force, it does not have to mean violence. This is not about violence versus nonviolence. Whether to wage your struggle using violent or nonviolent tactics is a decision that comes much later. Nonviolence is a very elegant political tactic when understood and used correctly. This is only to recognize that power is not a mistake, it's not a misunderstanding, it's not a disagreement. Justice is not won by rational argument, by personal transformation, or by spiritual epiphany. It's won by taking power away from the powerful and then dismantling their institutions.

So, the four categories of response. The first category of response is the legal one. Most activist groups naturally are drawn to the legal arena, and that's for a very good reason. As Catharine MacKinnon says, "Law organizes power." The trick is, we need to do this as radicals, and that means asking the questions: Does this initiative redefine power, not just who is at the top of the pyramid?

Does it take away the rights of the oppressors and reestablish the rights of the dispossessed? Does it let people control the material conditions of their lives?

Number two is direct action. Other activists will bypass that legal arena altogether and go for other ways to apply pressure. A great example from history is the Montgomery bus boycott. People used their economic power. They boycotted the bus for eighteen months and brought the bus company to its knees. But as with legal remedies, direct action can be anywhere from liberal to downright revolutionary.

The third category is withdrawal. The main difference between withdrawal as a successful strategy and withdrawal as a failed strategy is whether the withdrawal is seen as adequate in itself or whether it's linked to political resistance. This difference hinges exactly on that distinction between the liberal and the radical. Issues of identification and loyalty are crucial to resistance movements. It's important to build class consciousness. But this alone is not enough. Withdrawal has got to go beyond the intellectual, the emotional, the spiritual. It has to include a goal of actually bringing about justice. Withdrawal may give solace, but ultimately, it will change nothing. Living in a rarified bubble-world of the converted is a very poor substitute for freedom—and it will not save our planet.

Here's a quote by Gene Sharp, the foremost theorist on nonviolent direct action. He's been responsible for revolutions all over the world. The people that I call "withdrawalists," he calls "utopians." "Utopians are often especially sensitive to the evils of the world, and, craving certainty, purity, and completeness, they firmly reject the evil as totally as possible, wishing to avoid any compromises with them. They await a 'new world' which is to come into being by an act of God, a change in the human spirit, by autonomous changes in economic conditions, or by a deep spontaneous social upheaval— all beyond deliberate human control. The most serious weakness of this response to the problem of this world is not the broad vision, or the commitment of the people who believe in it. The weakness is that these believers have no effective way to reach the society of their dreams."

Well, that about sums up my youth. I've heard the phrase "secular millennialism." And that's exactly what Sharp is getting at.

The Left has these vague notions that our actions will inspire others and somehow accumulate into a societal transformation, or maybe kick off a spontaneous insurrection. There's the nonviolent version, which usually includes lifestyle choices like changes in diet, then there is militant action, like the approach taken by the Weather Underground. Those are the two poles of secular millennialism. Change will happen because it must: because either that "Great Turning" narrative of progress says that it must, or because the fires of our righteous rage will make it be so. But given that victory is not, in fact, inevitable, we would be well advised to understand the basic principle of resistance: dislodging injustice requires, in the words of Andrea Dworkin, "organized, political resistance."

The final category is spirituality. A withdrawalist stance is an answer to despair, but it is an answer that only relies on faith, so it's not a strategy—it's an emotional solution, not a material solution. And this merges into millenarianism, which is "any religious movement that predicts the collapse of the world order, replaced by this millennium, the period of justice, or equality, salvation."

There are a lot of examples from history of desperate people taking up millenarianism. Much of the Left has been infected with some version of this; people believe we can meditate to stop global warming, orgasm our way to peace, and if all else fails (which it will) there's always December 2012. Divine intervention has never yet stopped a system of unjust power. Across the entire sweep of human history, that is never. Material help from some other realm of existence is a very bad strategy. To date, it has been a complete failure.

This is not in any way to dismiss the role of spirituality in a true culture of resistance. Spirituality can give people the courage, endurance, and dignity that we need under oppressive conditions. It can also provide norms of behavior that help hold communities together under really rough situations. But faith is not a political strategy. The only miracle we're going to get is us.

Let's examine these ideas using an example from history: the Irish struggle for independence. The Irish had endured English occupation for eight hundred years, enduring the usual array of horrors. In 1880 came the birth of a new movement called the Gaelic Revival. This movement sought to bring cultural pride and self-respect to the Irish. They taught the language that was going extinct, and revived ancient traditions of theater, poetry, music, dance. In addition, groups like the Gaelic Athletic Association organized traditional Gaelic sports. Participants did more than just playing games: they learned how to work as a team, they learned about basic military strategy, and they learned to value physical fitness. The Gaelic Athletic Association went on to become the seed for the Irish Republican Brotherhood, which ultimately became the original IRA—which went on to wage the armed struggle.

The Gaelic Revival segued right into the first round of the struggle, called the Land War, which was a struggle to win back the land because Ireland was suffering from mass starvation. The Land War was tremendously successful. By 1914, 90 percent of the land was once again in the hands of the small- to medium-sized farmers, and it was all done almost entirely using nonviolent tactics.

So the pattern went like this: the Irish had a culture of resistance. Then the activists started achieving smaller goals, like winning the Land War. From there, the Irish were ready for actual armed resistance.

Again, it all started with the Gaelic Revival, with that culture of resistance. Nobody said, "Well, we'll just put on some nice plays and we'll sing some of our own songs and the English will go away."

Nobody said, "Well let's change our consciousness—we don't need to change this corrupt and brutal arrangement of power. No, if we just love each other enough, that'll magically do the trick." No one suggested that withdrawal alone would be a sufficient strategy. The Irish culture believed in resistance, it prepared for resistance, it supported the resistance, and ultimately it planned for its success. The Irish supported political prisoners and provided all kinds of material support for families that were in distress—especially if the breadwinner was in jail. They set up their own court system to settle disputes, and they ultimately went on to wage both violent and nonviolent struggle against the English occupation. Many political movements have a very similar trajectory. The Harlem Renaissance and the Pullman Porters created the same kind of bridge between slavery and the Civil Rights Movement.

The part of withdrawal that's necessary is breaking through the psychology of the oppressed: the accommodation, the denial, the consent. That's crucial. Developing self-respect, loyalty to your own people, and class-consciousness is crucial. But it's not enough. It's necessary, but it's not sufficient. So why is so much of the Left insisting on withdrawalist strategies, personal solutions, and vague millennialism as a fallback, especially when the entire planet is at stake? We need a little more history here. As my ex says, history is the same characters, different costumes. We are about to find out exactly how right she is.

First, I have to apologize: this next section is entirely about European history. The reason I'm discussing Europe is because even in today's Left, white people are still hegemonic, and they control the norms of behavior. So no matter what culture of resistance you come from, you're going to be up against these same problems that have come through from European history.

There's a long history in Europe of political movements and dissenting groups. Some are more religious, some are more utopian. There are records of movements as far back as ancient

Greece, but we're going to start with the Romantic Movement, an artistic movement that began in the second half of the eighteenth century in Western Europe. It was in part a reaction to the Age of Enlightenment, which valued rationality. The ascendancy of science, the mechanistic reduction of the cosmos to a machine, started at that time. Up until that point, the leading image of the cosmos or the earth was a living body. But with the age of rationality, people began to view the whole universe as a clockwork machine that that could be figured out and taken apart. With this mentality came an industrial revolution, and as it gained strength, the commons were destroyed. So the wetlands, the rivers, the forests—they all began to fall. People were pushed off into terrible conditions in cities. Of course, this is still happening today. It's the same story everywhere.

In response to this, the Romantic Movement emerged with three themes: the evocation of the past, the heroic isolation of the individual, and respect for wild nature. Germany, in particular produced a lot of the art and the music of this movement. Romanticism joined forces with the nationalism that was just starting to evolve there, and Germans showed a new interest in folk culture and a longing for connection to the ancient land.

Out of this came another movement called the Lebensreform movement. This was a social movement that emphasized physical fitness and natural health. Proponents of Lebensreform valued connecting with nature and all sorts of political and lifestyle components that come with it: paganism, feminism, psychoanalysis, pacifism, yoga, and Eastern religions like Buddhism and Hinduism. The Lebensreform movement created their own schools, their own clinics, and intentional communities. Many notable leaders, writers, and artists, from Isadora Duncan to Leon Trotsky to Franz Kafka, passed through the Lebensreform world at some point. Gandhi, too, was interested in the Lebensreform. He set up a nature clinic in India.

Some of the Lebensreform adherents were schoolteachers in Berlin. They had their students spend time in nature, often taking them on hikes. The hikes extended into weekend trips. The weekend trips started to become a lifestyle, as the teenagers started to coalesce into their own subculture.

That brings us to the Wandervogel Movement. These young people embraced the natural, the rural, the emotional, the spontaneous. The Wandervogel movement was the origin of the Youth Hostel movement. Young people wandered around the German countryside taking over abandoned buildings. They sang folk songs, they experimented with fasting, raw foods, and vegetarianism, and they embraced ecological ideas. This was all before the year 1900. They were the anarchist vegan squatters of the age.

The connections between the Lebensreform, the Wandervogel youth, and the 1960s counterculture in this country are startlingly direct. For example, there are the artists Gusto Graser and—he has one name—Fidus. You look at their paintings and you'd think you were looking at album covers from 1968. But they were painting before 1900, and they were already using the peace sign. Gusto Graser was a mentor to Herman Hesse, who wrote in the 1920s, but his books were taken up by the Beatniks and then sold by the millions in the 1960s. And that's just one example.

Some of the Wandervogel were pacifists and draft resisters in World War I in Germany. Many emigrated to the United States to escape the draft, and a lot of them ended up in California. If you were going to worship the sun and experiment with nudity, you might prefer California over Minnesota, too. They came here and wrote books about fasting, sunbathing, vegetarianism, and so on.

The cultural influence of the Wandervogel continues unbroken to this day. It is an alternative culture. What we need is a culture of resistance. So what's the difference?

EARTH AT RISK

Alternative Culture versus Oppositional Culture

Alternative Culture	Oppositional Culture
Apathetic or hostile to concept of political engagement	Consciously embraces resistance
Change seen in psychological and cultural terms	Change seen in economic and political terms
Individual consciousness is the target	Concrete institutions are targeted
Adolescent values of youth movement	Adult values of discernment, responsibility
All authority is rejected out of hand	Legitimate authority is accepted and cultivated
Rejection of moral judgment	Strong moral code based on universal human rights
Attack on conventions • all boundaries are fair game • shock value	Attacks on power structures
Alienated individual valorized	Loyalty and solidarity valued
Goal is to feel intense, "authentic," unmediated emotions	Goals and adult concerns guide the community, socialize the young, enforce norms, participate in larger projects of righting the world
A politics of emotions in which feeling states outweighs effective strategy or tactics	A politics of community that values responsibility, mutual aid, work ethic—dependent on self-regulation of mature adults
Politics is who you are	Politics is what you do
Human relations are corrupted in the act of political resistance; only right consciousness can prevail	Human relations are corrupted by systems of power and oppression; justice must prevail even if it takes generations
Generalized withdrawal as strategy	Withdraw loyalty from systems of oppression and the oppressors but active engagement to stop injustice
Moral vigor of youth cut off from action • horizontal hostility • questions of in group/out group	Idealism tempered by experience
Cultural appropriation	Cultural reclamation and protection; cultural respect, political solidarity (allies)

When I created this chart, I realized I was examining an alternative culture that was created by the adolescent brain. In the year 1911 in Germany, there were more teenagers than there ever would be again. The Wandervogel got transplanted to the U.S., went dormant for about fifty years, started to pick up speed again with the Beatniks, and what happened in 1960? The United States had its own bumper crop of teenagers, and of course, this is the culture they were attracted to. It's a culture created by people exactly like them.

The differences between an alternative and an oppositional culture have been present for centuries. It's a split to the root between the Romantics and the resistance. Both start with a rejection of some part of the social order, but they identify their enemy differently, and from there they head in opposite directions.

Here's one way of figuring out where you fall: are you apathetic to political engagement, or do you consciously embrace resistance?

In the alternative culture, the focus is on individual change. That's a hallmark of liberalism. Only individuals can change, so individuals are the only worthy project for change. Injustice becomes an excuse for narcissism. The idea of "personal example" is seen as some kind of activism. This is where you get all the emphasis on things like your personal carbon footprint. Am I the only one who has noticed? The only time that men try to prove they're smaller is when they're comparing carbon footprints.

As a political strategy, "personal example" always fails. By their nature, agricultural societies are imperialist; they're based on drawdown. Civilization follows that same pattern of conquering all the outlying regions. Over and over, for ten thousand years, imperialistic cultures have invaded the territory of neighboring Indigenous Peoples. Some of those Indigenous Peoples have embodied the values that everyone in this room holds dear: they are sustainable, egalitarian, peaceful cultures. And in all that time, over all those invasions, the face-to-face example of a sustainable, egalitarian culture has never once changed the invading culture. It has never once brought on an epiphany in the invaders. That's *never once*, in ten thousand years. "Personal example" does not work. The dominant culture will not change because it beholds the beautiful nonviolent values that we hold in our hearts, and it will not change because it sees our life-affirming, free-range compost piles. There are no exceptions. We're going to have to give this one up.

The farthest extreme of individualism is when personal lifestyle becomes personal purity, and one's identity itself is declared some kind of political act. Subcultures that buy into this mentality start to feel like cults. Again, any strategy based on individual change is doomed to fail, because social subordination is not an individual condition. It's a class condition, it's a group condition, and it will only change by group effort.

The defining characteristic of an oppositional culture, on the other hand, is that it consciously claims to be the cradle of resistance. Where the alternative culture exists to create personal change, the oppositional culture exists to nurture a serious movement for political transformation. Members of an oppositional culture understand that concrete systems of power have to be dismantled, and that such a project will require tremendous courage, commitment, risk, and potential loss of life.

Liberalism and adolescence dovetail perfectly in this focus on the individual. The adolescent brain is still under construction. The areas responsible for impulse control, long-range planning, considering consequences, and managing emotional states—which is mostly the frontal lobes—go offline when you're a teenager. A person's sense of time isn't developed fully until we're twenty-one years old. Adolescents cannot understand cause and effect, and they can't do long-range planning. They don't understand the consequences. They're prone to risk-taking, impulsive behavior, anger, and overall emotional intensity.

Adolescence is also that phase of life when that question, "Who Am I?" takes on this tremendous importance. There's nothing wrong with that—it's your job when you're a teenager. You've got to figure out who you are. But it's problematic to have a culture created by teenagers as opposed to a true culture of resistance.

In alternative culture, the idea of authority is rejected outright, whereas a serious resistance movement would be training people for appropriate leadership roles in the movement. For the alternative culture, the enemy is seen as a constraining set of values. For an oppositional culture, the enemy manifests as material conditions and concrete systems of power.

On the alternative side, the main program is one of attacking boundaries, rather than injustice. And this has had serious consequences on the Left. The creators of this counterculture were not just any teenagers—they were privileged, and they were male. This has spelled disaster for women and girls. These are the boys who brought us porn culture, and we are now collectively saturated in sexual sadism.

Alienation may be a good place to start, but you can't stop there. Alienated individuals cannot build loyalty or solidarity. Politics is always a group project, and you do have to play well with others to make it work.

In the alternative culture, that adolescent concern of identity, of *who I am*, takes on a political importance that outweighs what one might actually do. The counterculture is a product of this psychology and that's where it has been permanently stuck. The concerns of adolescence—its gifts and its shortcomings—are the framework for the alternative culture. Those community norms, those habits of behavior, have become accepted across the Left in what Theodore Roszak called in 1968 a "progressive 'adolescentization' of dissenting thought and culture."

Take, for example, this great motto of the Wandervogel: *Our lack of purpose is our strength*. No joke. Same characters, different costumes: sixty years later, we got Abbie Hoffman, *Revolution for the Hell of It*.

Of course, there is also a positive side to including teenagers in a resistance movement. The gifts of youth include incredible moral vigor, courage, passion, idealism. Every movement needs an infusion of those gifts, regularly. Because by the time you're middle-aged, they've worn off, and you're tired.

Unfortunately, the alternative culture stops there. It stops that vigor from translating into effective action. And when you can't fight power, all you can fight is each other. This is what Florynce Kennedy called "horizontal hostility." We see this all the time, a feeding frenzy of ugly gossip and character assassination. In more militant groups, it takes the form of paranoid accusations. In the worst instances, groups encourage macho posturing, and it often ends with men shooting each other. Ultimately, those kinds of problems are caused by fighting horizontally rather than vertically. If the only thing we could change was ourselves, or if the best tactics for social change were lifestyle choices, then indeed, critiquing the minutiae of people's personal lives would seem like a righteous activity. But if it feels like you're back in junior high school, there is a reason.

I want to return to the Wandervogel. The Romantic Movement and the Wandervogel created an image of The Peasant as an authentic, antirational symbol, as a people close to nature. This is where we get the peasant blouses, which are still with us. The Wandervogel's idea of a peasant had nothing to do with actual peasants, who did exist in Germany at the time and could have used some solidarity.

Well, when the Wandervogel got transplanted to the United States, there weren't any peasants, so two groups got pressed into service and continue to be used by the privileged for their own psychological needs: African Americans and Native Americans. These groups get cast as emotional, childlike, natural, authentic. So on the alternative side, cultural appropriation is the norm. On the oppositional side, that would be completely unacceptable.

Derrick: How do cultures of resistance work intergenerationally?

Lierre: In many resistance movements, the resistance quickens when the people over thirty have laid a lot of the groundwork, often for a generation or two. During the Civil Rights Movement, those who were part of the Harlem Renaissance and the Pullman Porters took a culture of survival and started to transform it into a culture of resistance. They accumulated self-respect, cultural pride, political experience, and material resources. All four of those are necessary, like laying up the firewood.

And someone has to light the match. In the Civil Rights Movement, that was the four college students who sat down at lunch counters and kicked the whole thing off. The original four who started were all eighteen-year-old college freshmen. And on March 2, 1955, Claudette Colvin refused to give up her seat on the bus to a white man and was dragged from the bus by the police. She was fifteen years old. A few months later, Mary Louise Smith did the same thing. She was eighteen years old. Finally, December 1, Rosa Parks famously did it again. The third time was the charm.

The number of teenagers involved is never a coincidence. It's always the young who strike that match. In the Civil Rights Movement, there were even younger kids in the Children's Crusade. The world was horrified by pictures of policemen turning fire hoses on twelve-year-olds. And then there were even younger kids. And there was little Ruby Bridges, who single-handedly desegregated the Louisiana public school system. We really have no right to be standing on the sides wringing our hands about how we can't do anything, when a six-year-old could produce that kind of courage.

The British Suffragists followed a similar pattern. There were three generations of people fighting for abolition, for labor, for women's suffrage. Emmeline Pankhurst was one of the leaders of the movement. She had *Uncle Tom's Cabin* read to her as a bedtime story. She wrote, "Young as I was—I could not have been older than five years—I knew perfectly well the meaning of the words 'slavery' and 'emancipation.'" Now that's a culture of resistance. In turn, her daughters Christabel and Sylvia grow up in the struggle. They used to cry because they were too young to go to meetings. They wanted to go so badly. At one point, young Christabel said to her mom, "How long you women have been trying for the vote. For my part, I mean to get it." And her mother was actually quite afraid of her daughters' fearlessness. She wrote in her journal, "Was there a difference between trying for the vote and winning the vote?" And she realized that if she could bring together the experience of the older women with that passion and fearless idealism of the young, she could create a movement that would actually work.

She was absolutely right. She created the Women's Social and Political Union, the WSPU. They performed massive, relentless civil disobedience, including hunger strikes in prison, where they were tortured. Parliament passed a law specifically so that they could be tortured. It even used the female pronoun—the prisoner, "she"—just in case anybody was unclear on the concept. When the civil disobedience stopped working, Christabel escalated the troops to arson. They blew up mailboxes, golf courses, historic buildings, railway stations. The dress reform movement hadn't gotten very far, so they were wearing forty pounds of skirting in addition to corsets. They couldn't breathe, and they were running through fields in the middle of the night being chased by police, scaling walls, carrying bombs. And they did it. Gandhi was a big fan of the WSPU. He subscribed to three different British newspapers so he could keep up on their actions. The Pankhursts were brilliant strategists, and they were loved by their movement.

Contrast that to now, when the Left has a terrible tendency to cannibalize its leaders. That was not always the case. People went to extraordinary lengths to protect the Pankhursts from jail. So the current cannibalism of leaders on the Left has everything to do with those cultural norms created by the teenagers, that knee-jerk reaction now against all authority.

So resistance movements always need a constant infusion of courage and idealism from the young. Resistance movements don't get anywhere without that. But they also need the experience, the stability, and the material resources, combined with the long-range planning, that adults are capable of. The real point here is that successful resistance movements are always multigenerational. Breaking the natural bonds between the young and the old means that political wisdom never accumulates. What it means now, especially, is that the young aren't socialized into a culture of resistance. They are being socialized instead into this pretty horrifying popular culture created by corporate America, which has everything to gain by destroying our capacity for community, never mind our capacity for resistance.

Are we after shock value or are we after justice? Is the problem a constraining set of values, or an oppressive set of material conditions? Are we content to coexist alongside injustice in all its horrors, no matter how repelled we are by those horrors? Is the self really an appropriate long-term project, or can we move on to something a little bit bigger now? Because another two hundred species went extinct today and they were my kin.

Derrick: So what do we need?

Lierre: We need organized political resistance. The task of an activist is not to navigate around systems of oppression with as much personal integrity as possible, it's to dismantle those systems. Consumer choices, spiritual choices, lifestyle choices—those are not going to dismantle global arrangements of power. That's the problem.

To get to a real resistance, we need a culture of resistance. Instead, we have the permaculture wing, we have the transition towners, the voluntary simplicity people. I call them the OIMBYs—Only In My Back Yard. Taken as a whole, they—with some exceptions—dismiss political action as either impractical or impossible. This is a very bad habit that the Left is going to have to break. We are the people who should be shouting from every street corner and every rooftop that not only is resistance possible, *failure* is impossible, given what's at stake.

So let's pretend that we're in Nazi-occupied France, or U.S.-occupied Viet Nam, or even U.S.-occupied North America, for that matter. Would anyone really suggest that riding bikes and buying organic shampoo would drive them out and win our freedom? I get that we have an emotional block. It's hard to name a perpetrator. I understand that. But they do have names and addresses, and more importantly, the infrastructure of industrial civilization is incredibly vulnerable.

So how would a resistance movement be organized today? Throughout history, the culture of resistance has built the new institutions that can take over and organize that better society as the old ones come down. Meanwhile, combatants have direct confrontations with those in power. Again, when I say combatants, that does not have to mean violence. The distinction is not between violence and nonviolence. The distinction is between doing something and doing nothing, between fighting power and submitting to power.

We need large numbers of people who can do the standard work that cultures of resistance do: setting up local economies that are just and sustainable, setting up participatory democracy, creating systems of justice for settling disputes, promoting character-building, breaking through the denial, the accommodation, the consent, and then providing direct support for the frontline resistance.

The vast majority of people are not going to resist shit. And I think we have to accept that. Of those that do, it will still be only a tiny number that ever take up those frontline positions. That's true in regular armies—only 2 percent of people in the Army ever take up combat roles; the other 98 percent provide the support. It was true in the IRA—2 percent were all that ever picked up weapons; 98 percent provided the support. Most people don't have the personality for frontline positions, or they can't take the risks for very legitimate reasons. And that's fine, because we do need the support roles filled.

But the rest of this is for you who *are* the 2 percent. You are the people I want to talk to. Because we need warriors who will put themselves between what is left of this planet and fossil fuel. We need to stop industrial civilization. Now, that could be done non-violently. If we had the numbers we could bring this party down by midnight using human blockades. I don't see the numbers. I would love to be wrong. I would vastly prefer to wage this struggle using nonviolence, but I don't see the numbers, and my longing will not bring them forth. And it's a little late in the day for millennialism.

Given a realistic assessment of what we actually have, the only viable strategy left that I can see is direct attacks on infrastructure. In the plainest terms: we need to stop them.

This is not a game for children, and this revolution is not for the hell of it. We need a serious underground organization that has the training, the discipline, the command structure, and the strategic savvy to coordinate decisive action on a continental scale. We needed it yesterday. And it would be really great if the permaculture wing could get on board and provide that loyalty and material support. At the very least, they've got to stop saying that this can't be done. It can. The only real question is, why aren't we doing it? I hate that part of the answer is because we are the people who benefit from this repulsive arrangement of power.

Not only can it be done, there are manuals that will tell you how. They are written with your tax dollars. You might as well read them.

We need to learn these principles of asymmetric warfare—and if there was ever an asymmetric conflict, this is it.

Decentralized Execution. "Guerrilla combat operations feature centralized planning and decentralized execution." So we need to coordinate to build toward those long-range goals, those long-term objectives. We need intelligence and planning.

Surprise is one of our only advantages, because the enemy has all the resources.

We want **Short Duration Action.** This means accomplishing our objectives swiftly, then disappearing. This is not a pitched battle. We would never win. They've got everything.

Finally, we aim for coordinated, **multiple attacks** using surprise; what we're ultimately after is cascading systems failure.

The point is not to make a statement. The point is to make a decisive material impact. In other words: we bring it down.

The reason you can learn about asymmetric warfare at places like West Point, and the U.S. Army, and training camps all around the world, is because direct attacks on infrastructure are highly effective as a strategy. The principles have been honed for decades. When understood and used properly, asymmetric warfare is highly effective. So please stop saying that it doesn't work.

We should select our targets using the following criteria:

- **Criticality.** How important is this?
- **Vulnerability.** How tough is your target?
- **Accessibility.** How easy is it to get near the target?
- **Recuperability.** What would it take to replace this, or repair it?

And suddenly there are a few things that start to make sense. One reason that groups like the ELF have had no decisive success is because their targets have low criticality, high recuperability. That is very typical for resistance groups that lack training. Targets are chosen for their accessibility—they're easy to get to—but they're not in any way critical, and they are easily repaired. This would be your basic McDonalds window strategy—and I say this as someone who has smashed her share of windows. I have personally destroyed thousands of dollars of property. It is a lot of fun, but ultimately, it's pointless. Why? Low criticality, high recuperability. Smashing that window does not stop the Bad People from doing their Bad Things for even a second.

We have to stop thinking like vandals and start thinking like field commanders. We've been carrying out operations that are emotionally appealing in the hopes that they would somehow accumulate into an effective action. I call this emotional activism, and it merges well with secular millennialism. This was the problem, for instance, with the Weather Underground. Increasing your firepower will not increase the soundness of your strategy.

You're not going to walk away from this with a serious grounding in the theory and practice of guerrilla warfare. But this is my point: other people have figured this out, serious people, people who intend to win. They have a goal, a grand strategy, and after examining the resources they actually have on hand, they move on to tactics.

So I'd say we have a two-part goal.

- **Part 1:** To disrupt and dismantle industrial civilization; to thereby remove the ability of the rich to steal from the poor and the powerful to destroy the planet.
- **Part 2:** To defend and rebuild just, sustainable, and autonomous human communities; and as part of that, to assist in the recovery of the land.

These two goals are interdependent. The movements involved are going to have to work in tandem for either to be successful. That's why I want the permaculture wing to get on board. Part 2 is going to involve large numbers of people in many different organizations, operating completely aboveground. Part 1 could be achieved using nonviolent tactics, but we don't have the numbers, and I think we all know that. So we're going to need an underground network that's both well-trained and dead serious.

And in case you can't find a way to hope, there is hope.

The aboveground could take its hope from the French labor strike that happened in November 2010. The protestors used trucks, burning tires, and human blockades to stop the fuel depots, and they managed to close all twelve of France's oil refineries. The major oil terminal was offline for three weeks. They stranded thirty oil tankers out in the Mediterranean. When the government tried to open the country's emergency reserves, they escalated and the protestors blockaded twenty more terminals. In a few weeks, the entire economy was grinding to a halt for lack of fuel.

The French strikers did what every military and every insurgency does: they interrupted key nodes of infrastructure. They were well on their way to completely shutting down the economy, and they did it using nonviolence. So it could be done. If we had the bodies, it could be done. The question is: do we?

That's for the aboveground.

For the belowground, your hope is MEND, the Movement for the Emancipation of the Niger Delta. The oil industry has earned hundreds of billions of dollars from Nigeria's oil. Oil accounts for 40 percent of the country's Gross Domestic Product. The Niger Delta is the world's largest wetland, only now it could more readily be called a sludgeland. The Indigenous people used to be able to support themselves. No more. They're now knee-deep in the oil industry waste. The fish have been devastated, the people are sick and starving. The original resistance was MOSOP, and this was led by the poet-activist Ken Saro-Wiwa. Theirs was a nonviolent campaign against Royal Dutch/Shell and the military regime. In 1995, Saro-Wiwa and eight others, the leaders of this movement, were all hanged by the military, despite international outcry and despite their nonviolence. And by all accounts Ken Saro-Wiwa was hanged last, which is to say he had to watch all his friends die first. So, in case you had any questions about the sadism of the people that we are fighting, there it is.

MEND is the second generation resistance. They do direct attacks against infrastructure—bridges, office sites, storage facilities, rigs, pipelines, and the support vessels. They have reduced Nigeria's oil output by a third. In one single attack, they were able to stop 10 percent of the oil output and in a series of attacks in December 2010, right before Christmas, they stopped 80 percent of the oil in one week. Their main tactic is the use of speedboats in surprise attacks against simultaneous targets. They're constantly working toward that goal of cascading systems failure. These people are quite serious. They're very sophisticated, they have university educations, they've studied other militant movements. Their training in combat is so good that they have fought and won in skirmishes against both Nigeria's elite fighting forces and Shell's private military.

Did you know oil companies have their own private militaries? I don't know where people in the United States think oil comes from. You can't grow it in the back yard. It doesn't fall from the sky like rain. It has to be ripped out of the land. And that means that people have to be ripped off their land. And that means those people have to be ripped in half. And that is done by private militaries.

According to the Council on Foreign Relations, MEND has "broad sympathy among the Niger Delta community." This sympathy has helped them maintain security. People take them in, but they don't turn them in. These are not armed thugs. This is a true resistance movement. And they number just a few hundred.

So understand: a few hundred people, well-trained and organized, have reduced the oil output of Nigeria by a third. MEND has said to the oil industry, "It must be clear that the Nigerian government cannot protect your workers or assets. Leave our land while you can or die in it." I can guarantee that everyone here has more resources than everyone in MEND put together when they started. Resistance is not just theoretically possible. It's happening now. The question is: are we going to join them? What if we said, "Leave our land or you will die in it?" What if we meant it?

The facts as they stand: Our planet is dying. Actually, she's being drawn and quartered. We are on the verge of complete biotic collapse. There are parts of China where there are no longer any flowering plants. No flowering plants. It's because the pollinators are all dead. That is five hundred million years of evolution, gone. Complete biotic collapse. We are out of soil, we are out of species, and we are out of time. And catastrophic climate change has already begun.

We really need to start thinking like a serious resistance movement. Because this is a war. I know it's been going on for ten thousand years, and it feels like daily life. The lights are on and the cupboards are full, but this is a war. And if anyone is left to look back a hundred years from now, they are going to wonder what the fuck was wrong with us that we didn't fight like hell when our planet was going down.

You love something, or you wouldn't be here. Whatever you love, it is under assault. Love is a verb. We have to let that love call us to action.

Stephanie McMillan

"What's missing in our movement is the understanding that if we are to radically transform social relations and the way we meet our needs as a society, then we need to rupture the economic cycle. We have to dispossess the dispossessors, and take back our means of subsistence."

Derrick Jensen: Stephanie McMillan is an award-winning cartoonist with a daily comic strip called *Minimum Security*. She is the author of a number of comic books and graphic novels, including *The Beginning of the American Fall: A Comics Journalist Inside the Occupy Wall Street Movement* and *As the World Burns: 50 Simple Things You Can Do to Stay in Denial*. She is also an organizer for One Struggle, an anti-capitalist/anti-imperialist collective.

Stephanie McMillan: We have an enemy: the social/economic/political/cultural system that's dominating and destroying the planet. We'll have to defeat it. Ultimately, that will require revolution. Right now, our main weapon is information. Before we can defeat our enemy, we have to correctly identify it. We have to understand how it works, who controls it, and its underlying structure in order to pinpoint its vulnerabilities and work out effective strategies of intervention.

I've been an activist since the early 1980s. All this time, a serious weakness of the environmental and social justice movements has been a lack of understanding of the nature of our enemy. Even in today's Occupy mobilizations, there's an overall reluctance to name the system that's dominating the planet. Instead we hear vague populist terms like "The 1 percent," "the rich," "banksters," and "greedy corporations."

Your work, Derrick, has been an incredible breakthrough in exposing people to the idea that civilization is at the foundation of structures of domination. Now I'd like to dig into the mechanisms of the current form of civilization, which is global capitalism.

Many activists don't know how capitalism actually functions. We have to understand *why* it's structurally impossible to reform, so that we can deal with the necessity—and our responsibility—not to fix it (because oppression is built into it from the start) but to do away with it, and to figure out all that will entail. We may in fact be the last generation with the opportunity to do this.

Derrick: We're certainly the last generation with the opportunity to do this.

Stephanie: And without digging under the surface to understand the system's true nature, it'll defeat us every time.

Derrick: Can you give me an example of that?

Stephanie: I experienced it, not for the first time, unfortunately, last year with the BP oil spill.

When the spill happened, I attended a spontaneous demonstration in front of a neighborhood BP station, holding a sign in the hot sun—which I got tired of in five minutes. I've done my time holding signs on sidewalks, and it didn't accomplish anything before, and it wasn't accomplishing anything this time. BP was still setting oil-covered sea turtles on fire and spraying Corexit into the water.

Derrick: As we speak, dolphins are washing up on the shores of the Gulf of Mexico, dead, at a rate of four to five times the normal rate.

Stephanie: It's an ongoing atrocity. So I decided to strategize with a few local activists to come up with something more effective. We called for an open meeting to form a coalition to shut down BP and stop offshore oil drilling, and we publicized it. That seems like a common-sense approach, but it was a mistake.

The system has many methods of dealing with dissent. One is open repression. But before they resort to that, they try everything else, including coopting it. The system draws dissent into dead ends it creates for this purpose: pressuring public officials, working with corporate and state funded nonprofits, exercising formal civil rights such as free speech. As long as we don't threaten the actual relationship of power, we have all these means of dissent that we're permitted to exercise. And because the system employs ideological hegemony (in other words, brainwashing), most people can't conceptualize resistance outside of this framework allowed by the system itself. Spontaneously, they follow the paths that have been laid out for them.

The first meeting had fifty people, which I initially thought was great. About 10 percent were a variety of radicals; the rest were either longtime liberal activists or those who had never done anything political before but were outraged about the spill.

It seemed like a viable ratio. I figured that radicals could function as one trend within a diverse range. The problem was, we hadn't organized as radicals going into it. We didn't know each other very well, or have a plan. So what ended up happening was that radical approaches were ignored in favor of responses that the majority believed were open to them: to protest at a congressperson's office; to help a liberal commissioner get elected; to invite institutional environmental groups for yet another protest on the sidewalk, with signs reading "Clean Energy Now"; and to present public talks by "green" businesses.

One radical immediately saw where this was going, and walked out in the middle of the first meeting. By the third or fourth meeting, all the rest were gone. The collective demand shifted from stopping BP and all offshore drilling to one more "realistic": a demand for safer valves on oilrigs. Finally, the group adopted the name "Clean Energy Coalition" and decided to plant a tree at a church.

There's absolutely nothing wrong with planting a tree at a church. It's a very good thing to do. But it doesn't stop BP, much less challenge the system that allows entities like BP to destroy the planet.

I learned several lessons.

1.   In society overall and thus at any open gathering, the default majority doesn't grasp the system's unreformable structure, or identify it as the enemy. Thus, they will not oppose it in any fundamental sense. So liberal and reformist ideas will tend to overwhelm the more radical ones.
2.   Individual radicals have little power. We need to be organized autonomously to exert collective influence within larger formations.
3.   There's an essential difference between mobilizations and movement building. Mobilizations aren't that difficult: when some new outrage occurs, issue a call and a bunch of angry people might come out. They don't have to agree on much. But when they go home again, we end up with nothing. We need organizations resilient enough to withstand the inevitable ebbs and flows of mass struggles.

Derrick: What did you do after that?

Stephanie: I connected with other local radicals and we formed a collective, called One Struggle. Now we can assert a radical presence when working with other groups and coalitions. We even worked with the Clean Energy Coalition and other groups to hold a rally, during which we distributed our own materials. We can organize independently within other mobilizations, such as the Occupy upsurge, and grow stronger even if that dissipates.

Derrick: Let's go back to global capitalism. How would you define it?

Stephanie: It's an economic system characterized by commodity production and private appropriation, in which one section of people monopolizes the means of subsistence, and the others are forced to sell their labor to survive.

Economic class divisions emerged about ten thousand years ago, roughly in tandem with agriculture. From the beginning, class-divided economies (which I see as roughly corresponding to civilization itself) have been organized around the private appropriation of "surplus" wealth, accomplished through the production of storable, exchangeable goods: salt, coffee, iPads, cars, grains, and so on. The flow of commodities from earth to assembly line to land fill is the basis of, and is represented by, the circulation and accumulation of a very abstract form of wealth, which is money.

Capitalism is, on the one hand, a social relation, whereby one economic class—a small minority, the ruling class—dominates all others. On the other hand it's a process: the endless flow of money to commodity production for another generation of money. But it's not linear; it's both cyclical and progressive, like a spiral.

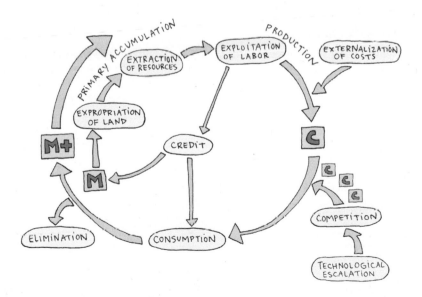

Here's an extremely simplified and necessarily incomplete representation of capitalism's basic structure. Since this is a cycle—the original vicious cycle—we can start at any point. Let's start with M: money. Say a bank or a queen or anyone who already has surplus wealth extends a line of credit to some explorer to gather a group of armed thugs, go out into the world, locate wealth and steal it. The first part of the process is primary accumulation, where land is expropriated and resources are extracted.

The expropriation of land does a few things. The conqueror can use that land and extract whatever is in and on it. And as the people are dispossessed—no longer able to live on the land—they're forced into labor camps (commonly known as cities). They become dependent on jobs. This is how the working class is created and continuously resupplied. It also creates the consumer: without land, we have to pay for food, shelter, and all our other needs.

The next part is production. One of the defining features of capitalism is the exploitation of labor. Exploitation has a precise meaning in economics, which isn't simply using someone for material gain. It means the worker is paid less than the exchange value of what they produce. During the time that they're paid $10, they might make items worth $100. That extra $90, minus fixed costs, is surplus value that the capitalist privately appropriates—in other words, steals.

Externalization of costs is another way the capitalist commits theft, and murder as well. Pollution from the production process is discharged into the environment. The numerous and serious consequences, never mind the cleanup which never happens, are not paid for by the capitalist who caused the problem, but by society as a whole, and by every living being on earth.

Derrick: Researchers at Cornell University say that 40 percent of all human deaths—twenty-three million per year and sixty-three thousand per day—are caused by water, air, and soil pollution.

Stephanie: If it's true of humans, then it's likely true of all creatures.

Other capitalists are running this same cycle. All their commodities flow into the marketplace. Competition is the major economic driving force of capitalism. Capitalists compete against each other for the sale by out-marketing each other or by undercutting each other in price. This puts pressure on the rate of profit to fall. To remain competitive, the capitalists are forced to cut costs (especially wages, the largest variable cost in most businesses), and they're forced to escalate productivity, which drives technological development in search of efficiency and speed.

Smaller companies that can't keep up are driven out of business or bought up by larger ones, forming monopolies in certain sectors. Four companies control 90 percent of the world's grain production. Only ten to twelve produce most semiconductors. Ten produce most pharmaceuticals. These monopolies can control prices to counteract the falling rate of profit. So while the local hardware store is failing, large oil companies are making more money than ever.

The surplus value, or profit, created in production is locked inside the commodity until the moment of consumption. When you plunk your dollars down to buy the hair dryer or the box of frozen waffles, the capitalist's goal is realized.

Now we run into capitalism's major contradiction. Because the workers are collectively paid less than the total worth of commodities that they produce, there will always be more on the market than what can be consumed by the domestic population. This causes what's called the crisis of overproduction. There's too much stuff, and because profit is created by exploiting labor, the people will never—can never—be paid enough to buy it all.

The system can't absorb all that surplus value. What do they do with it? They can't just leave it lying around to depreciate; they have to get rid of it somehow. A portion is siphoned off for personal use by capitalists, to furnish extravagant lifestyles with excessive salaries and bonuses. They must force open more markets, one of the driving forces for imperialism. Some of the surplus is simply thrown away, eliminated through waste, wars, and so-called international "aid." The latter two also function as centers for creating even more profit, which capitalists pursue, but which also exacerbates the overall problem. Finally, they increase the level of consumption with infusions of credit, basing the consumer economy on debt. Of course this creates bubbles and instability, which grow progressively worse.

Back at the start, surplus value has to be reinvested. It must be more than they started with, because only through expansion can each company gain a competitive edge over all the others. For capitalism to function, it must grow about 3 percent annually. So the cycle goes around again, but bigger. In the next turn, they must extract more raw materials, exploit more labor, manufacture more products, generate more waste, make more profits. This isn't easy; as economies become saturated, there's less opportunity for profitable investment. So they have to invent ways to turn more things into commodities, invading us through privatization and monetizing every aspect of our lives, from our emotions to genetic material.

As we know, you can't have infinite growth on a finite planet. Today the crisis of overproduction has become acute, and the system is maxed out. It's reaching the end of all physical limits. Last year, David Bianco, the head of U.S. equity strategy at Bank of America, said: "Cash is piling up faster than companies can figure out what to do with it."

Derrick: You know, I've long had that problem myself.

Stephanie: They deserve our deepest sympathy.

U.S. corporations are sitting on $1.6 trillion in cash. Apple alone has $76.4 billion, a larger amount than the U.S. government has in reserve. They're desperate to invest it, but there's nowhere profitable to put it. Tycoons like Warren Buffett and Bill Gates are begging to be taxed and are giving away billions of dollars. Of course philanthropy generates profits, too, so the system ends up further saturated. The machine is grinding to a halt.

Derrick: Does this mean capitalism will collapse on its own?

Stephanie: Unfortunately, not soon enough. Capitalism in crisis becomes even more ruthless, as we see with extreme extraction like oil from tar sands and fracking for natural gas. They no longer even bother to keep up the pretense of caring about the future. Capitalism will ultimately destroy itself, but only when it's destroyed all life on the planet, which is too late to matter. Until then, capitalism is all about breaking through limitations. That's what it always does.

Derrick: How can they expand beyond physical limits?

Stephanie: Increasingly, capitalists are busting through the over-production problem by bypassing the production process altogether. Instead, they use money to make more money, through interest on credit, speculation, and arbitrage. This seems to throw production—along with workers and consumers—out of the equation. Though commodity production is still the largest part of the global economy, it's declining in the U.S. In the early 1970s, the U.S. produced 38 percent of the world's commodities; today it's only 9 percent. Six million manufacturing jobs have vanished since the year 2000. In contrast, finance capitalism is on the rise: in 1978, 2 percent of global profit came from finance. Today it's 42 percent. So its influence on the economy is considerable, and destabilizing. But producing more commodities is destabilizing, too. So the crisis shifts from place to place, with no long-term, workable options.

This escape from production is partial and temporary and will inevitably crash, because the money isn't based on real things. It's fake surplus value. It's gambling on bad debt and toxic assets. There's nothing underpinning it. Financial collapse has happened many times before, and it will again. It'll cause chaos and shakeups. Major business interests will fail. On the negative side will be the increased suffering of the majority of people who are trapped inside the economy. Plus we may see the rise of fascism, and the conflict between industrial and financial sectors may even break out into civil war. But for the ruling class as a whole, this will bring a certain salvation, an opportunity for the system to restructure itself. There will be an economic lurch downward to "reset" to a level that will spark a new round of the accumulation process, once again based on the production of material commodities that contain real surplus value.

Derrick: Why can't they work together to solve their crisis without all the destruction? Why don't they invest their extra capital in positive projects, such as land rehabilitation, or provide jobs so the people don't revolt?

Stephanie: They can cooperate to a certain degree, and they do, but capital has a motion of its own beyond the interests of individual capitalists. Competition is the primary mechanism of the economy, and it's the reason the system can't be reformed, even to save the capitalists themselves. Capitalists must go after the most accessible profits, no matter how irrationally they're obtained, and regardless of their personal desires. They can't care whether or not what's produced is useful or good. For destroying the environment to maximize profits, executives get promoted. For changing their policies out of concern for the environment, and making less profit, they'd be replaced.

Massive unemployment really isn't a problem for the ruling class. If they create more jobs, the problem of overproduction would actually get worse. But high unemployment and cuts in social programs work out quite nicely for them, because soon we'll be screaming for jobs and willing to accept any pathetic wages.

Factoring in the costs of transporting goods, the wages of workers in China and the U.S. are reaching parity. When that happens we'll see a resurgence of domestic production here, but reset at a lower level. These won't be union jobs allowing decent living conditions, and forget health care. Watch for the elimination of the minimum wage. They'll say, "We're very sorry; it's only a temporary measure for your sake, to bring jobs back to the U.S."

Derrick: That's a good sound bite. Are you running for Republican presidential nomination?

Stephanie: No, I said, "We're very sorry." That means I'm working for Obama.

This is in store for us whether or not cheap oil runs out. Capitalists don't care where they get their energy—coal, natural gas from fracking, oil from tar sands and the deep oceans, biofuels, solar, wind, algae, and even slave labor. The sources don't matter as long as they control it all. The system is dynamic, adaptable, and infinitely ruthless. It will not collapse by itself. There's no escape from our need to destroy it.

Derrick: Why do people put up with this miserable nightmare?

Stephanie: Because of the superstructure: the ideas and institutions that we can picture as a shell around the economic structure, both supporting it and shaped by its needs. The sole purpose of the state is to keep the flow of capital running smoothly. It administers and regulates the process with its government and legal system. It enforces it with its military, police, prison complex, and security apparatus.

The culture also serves capitalist interests. The only ideas allowed to participate in the market are prosystem; any others are starved of support. The dominant culture tells us how to think and behave through the stories and myths of mainstream media, entertainment, and religion. It indoctrinates us in its schools. Its traditions

train us in habits of obedience to authority and individualism. Its
ideologies reinforce structural oppression such as misogyny, racism,
homophobia, and xenophobia. The nuclear family is a self-policing
social unit enforcing the domination of children and women.

We need to break through this superstructure to choke off the
flow of capital.

Derrick: How?

Stephanie: There are so many possibilities. Because we don't know,
until they happen, which contradictions or crises will create revolutionary openings, we have to be prepared to intervene everywhere.
Significant attention must be focused at the economic nodal points,
because a revolutionary movement must be able to damage, weaken,
and ultimately halt capital's flow. Of primary importance right now is
helping people understand why this system needs to be taken down,
and how their various social and political struggles are connected at
this foundational point.

This is so crucial because the system has numerous methods of
assimilating our struggles, and we have to make sure we don't get
sidetracked. It diverts discontent into forms that reinforce its own
institutions. These are very sophisticated and persuasive; they make
people feel that they are making a difference, when in fact they're
tightening the bonds of their own oppression.

Elections, corporate-funded nonprofits, NGOs and CBOs, personal change, political pressure, culture-jamming, tinkering with the
economy, green jobs, withdrawing our support, symbolic protests—
all are offered up as options for dissent. None of them are sufficient;
on the contrary, they serve to reinforce the system's authority and the
illusion of democracy. These approaches have traction because most
people don't grasp how the system actually works, and that it's structurally unreformable. They don't recognize it as the absolute enemy
that it is. What's missing in our movement is the understanding that

if we are to radically transform social relations and the way we meet our needs as a society, then we need to rupture the economic cycle. We have to dispossess the dispossessors, and take back our means of subsistence.

Derrick: If we begin to accomplish that, then won't the capitalists just put us in prison or kill us?

Stephanie: They will try. A revolutionary movement is going to have to fight—and defeat—their armed forces and overthrow their state, in order to break the shell to get to the economic core.

Waging a revolution means going to war with the capitalist class. I mean "war" in the most difficult and challenging sense—not a PR war, not a war for hearts and minds, but a war for power. As long as capitalists possess the power to expropriate and exploit, they will not stop. There's no avoiding it. The blood of our people—the dispossessed and exploited all over the world—is already spilled daily as part of the ordinary workings of capitalism. Our sisters and brothers are fighting and dying in struggle against the same enemy, and our expressions of solidarity mean nothing unless we're striving as hard as we can to build our capacity so we can one day—as soon as possible—fight alongside them.

Obviously, and sadly, we aren't in a position to do this yet. A people's army without a strong mass movement to back it up is a suicide squad, and can't possibly win. People have tried this already; let's not waste the hard-won experience of the Red Army Faction or the George Jackson Brigade. Today, our task is to increase our capacity, to build the organizations that together can be powerful enough to overcome the capitalist's accumulated forces of lies, wealth, and arms.

Derrick: What kind of organizations are you talking about, and how do you see building them?

Stephanie: Here's what my comic strip character Bunnista says about that.

Indeed, this isn't going to be easy. We can't conjure this movement out of thin air, and it won't be exactly what we want or think we need. It will emerge from our current reality, flawed, chaotic, and largely unpredictable. It's not going to follow any formula, but we aren't flying completely blind either. Worldwide we have a rich history of resistance and revolutionary theory to draw from.

Because of the particular history and culture of the U.S., we can't expect, at least in the initial stages, to be able to build one coherent movement that unites everyone. No single particular grouping is going to have sufficient theoretical understanding, mass support, and combative strength. But when we look at all the diverse forces in aggregate, the picture changes. Some combination of the various forces that are gelling into a resistance movement may be able to succeed.

Let's look at some of the issues where struggle is occurring now.

REFORM · RADICAL · REVOLUTIONARY

- LAND DEFENSE
- LABOR
- ANTI-OPPRESSION
- ANTI-IMPERIALISM/WAR
- CONSUMER ISSUES
- FINANCIAL ISSUES/DEBT

The shades represent different levels of consciousness within each struggle.

Revolutionaries understand the need to defeat those in power and transform social relations. Radicals understand the need to end the system. Reformers work for change within the context of the system. While each struggle and level is incomplete on its own, each can contribute to overall success. Like members of an ecosystem, each fills an essential niche. These trends must find ways to ally and cohere in a multifaceted movement in which each part retains its autonomy, but together they are able to coordinate activities, or at least offer mutual support.

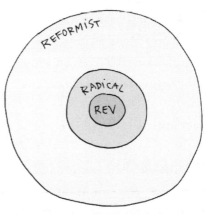

At the outer ring are reformers and liberals. This is where institutional unions, NGOs, politicians, the Democratic Party, and so on glom onto the movement to suck the life out of it, channeling activists into pointless and energy-draining losing strategies—which is their function. At the same time, a lot of people located there sincerely want change. We should encourage and assist combative mass organizations to fight for reforms that weaken capital, without sinking into reformism, an ideology that accepts the terms set by the ruling class. We should also strive to radicalize those we can (the continuing atrocities committed by the system will help with that more than anything), and provide alternatives to participate in. As for the liberals who can't be radicalized, when they're inevitably forced to take sides, we must insist upon their neutrality at the very least. Some will be tempted to betray the revolution in favor of the devil they know. We can't ignore them; if we don't attempt to win as many as possible over, fascists will do it.

Radicals can build a movement-within-a-movement that es-
tablishes, as a minimum point of unity, that our common enemy is
the system (whether we call it civilization, colonialism, imperialism,
or global capitalism), and encourages and challenges others to deal
with that reality. When broad sections of people are in motion, revolutionary organizations can also begin to congeal. At the core are
those who understand that this is a war for power, and develop corresponding strategies.

We should focus our energy on these center two rings. The
stronger their magnetic pull, the more they can draw others in from
the periphery. To add more weight there, we should work as close to
the center as we can get. For example, as a cartoonist I could organize
other cartoonists around free speech issues. But this is in the outer
zone of reform. There's nothing wrong with fighting for reforms, but
it's better to devote our energy to strengthening the center areas.

Derrick: Who would comprise a leading revolutionary core?

Stephanie: The sections of people capable of leading the revolutionary process, internationally, are collective or subsistence land-
based cultures resisting colonization and dispossession, and those
whose labor is exploited. Workers have been dispossessed of their
original means of subsistence, and are forced to sell their labor to the
capitalists to survive. For most of us, this happened so many generations ago that we no longer remember it. Indigenous societies either
haven't had this happen to them yet, or still remember that it did. Or
it's happening to them right now.

All of the dominated popular classes must wage struggle against
our common enemy. But for the revolution to achieve total liberation, it must be carried out under the leadership of the expropriated
and exploited. These two groups are strategically located where life is
converted to "surplus value." Capitalism cannot continue to function
if they're stopped from extracting "resources" or if laborers refuse to

work. The interests of Indigenous communities and the most exploited workers are diametrically opposed to capitalism; they come face to face with its most vicious forms, and their self-preservation depends on ending it. Plus, only they can lead society to a sustainable and classless way of life. Others will inevitably stop short.

Derrick: Where does saving the planet fit in?

Stephanie: The conversion of nature into commodities is intertwined with the exploitation of human labor; one can't happen without the other. Similarly, the fight to defend the land and traditional land-based ways of life is also connected to the fight for an end to exploitation, a classless society. One can't be won without the other. When we understand this, liberating ourselves and saving the planet become the same act.

Derrick: What about the fact that the environment and jobs are often viewed as conflicting, including by workers themselves?

Stephanie: No one would sell their labor—go willingly into a mine, factory, or cubicle day after day—if they still had the means to live otherwise. But capital has been very good at dividing the interests of the workers from the environment. This is, of course, intentional. After the Gulf oil spill, workers demanded that oilrigs open back up because they needed jobs to survive. Yet these are the very same people being poisoned by the externalization of costs. This is a bind that workers have been placed in. It can only be resolved by the overthrow of capitalism and taking back our means of subsistence. We don't need jobs at all—in fact, that just helps the capitalists. What we need is a sustainable way of life.

Two ideological elements are essential at the revolutionary core: biocentrism and class consciousness. Not everyone will start out with a full appreciation of both of these. But even if revolutionaries themselves don't yet realize it, these ideologies represent allied and complementary movements in a strategic sense. Each has its own strengths and weaknesses, each has gaps that are filled in by the other. They will have different strategies, but each will have better chances for success the more they cooperate.

The major flaw of the class struggle has been anthropocentrism, a total focus on human needs and a utilitarian view of nature.

The major flaw of environmentalists, and frankly, the labor movement as well (which has been mostly co-opted by sold-out unions) has been a lack of class analysis and understanding of capitalism as a system that we need to defeat. Instead, many fall victim to illusions of reformism, bourgeois democracy, technotopianism, lifestylism, and other bogus schemes. As the revolutionary project gains common experience, these movements will cross-pollinate, coming closer together in their struggles against their common enemy. It's the job of revolutionaries to foster unity between them, and the development of alliances.

As the economic and environmental crises converge, a mutual learning process in both directions is already beginning to occur. Defenders of labor and land are coming to grips with the gaps in their respective approaches, and are reaching out toward one another. Environmentalists are analyzing the underlying mechanisms that drive the system, connecting the fight to save the planet with social transformation, and beginning to build organizations capable of mass resistance. Communists and socialists are recognizing that the environmental crisis must be urgently addressed or there won't be a future at all. We see this cross-pollination spreading around the world.

Derrick: What should we do now to build the revolutionary movement?

Stephanie: We should build consciousness, organization, and struggle in a mutually reinforcing and escalating cyclical way.

First, revolutionary consciousness is foundational. Before it can happen in real life, revolution must first happen in the mind. Theory and ideological unity develop along with reality. Instead of dogmas and formulas, we need creativity and experimentation.

Second, we need to construct various forms of self-replicating, autonomous yet interconnected organizations. These ought to prefigure, as much as possible, a future sustainable and egalitarian society. Within our strategic alliances, diversity is our strength, and we need to be mutually supportive and set aside secondary conflicts and contradictions. We must maintain principled unity, even with people we don't particularly like.

Third, we need to engage in struggle. Knowledge doesn't come from teach-ins or study groups alone. We can't learn how to paint or play the guitar without practice; the same is true of revolution. We must take every opportunity to exercise our power against capital and its state apparatus, to the maximum extent possible at any given moment, with escalating intensity, until we're strong enough to defeat the capitalists, dismantle their system, and create an alternative.

There is a revolution struggling to come into being. It can only happen if we take responsibility for embodying it, giving it form by becoming, ourselves, revolutionary militants. Liberation is possible and, more to the point, necessary for the survival and well-being of all life on this earth.

Aric McBay

"Industrial collapse won't be easy, but it's better than a global ecological collapse. This culture is coming down anyway. If we engage with the process of collapse, we can guide it in a less destructive direction, rather than letting those in power have control."

Derrick Jensen: Aric McBay is a writer, activist, and small-scale organic farmer. His first book was *Peak Oil Survival: Preparation for Life After Gridcrash*. He's also the coauthor of *What We Leave Behind* and *Deep Green Resistance*.

Deep Green Resistance first came about when Aric, Lierre Keith, and I all happened to be in Maine, where I was doing an event. Before the event we were talking about the fact that as environmentalists we're losing badly on all fronts. All biological indicators, if I can use mechanistic language I hate, are going in the wrong direction. All natural communities are being destroyed. So we asked each other, what would actually work? What strategy would actually work to stop this culture from killing the planet? We had already tried a lot of strategies. We distributed online petitions, but that didn't work. So we graduated to electoral politics, and that didn't work. So we graduated to signs saying "Save the Earth Now." It didn't work. So that evening, we talked about what strategy would actually have a chance.

Environmentalists, for the most part, don't think strategically. What do we want? Do we want smaller clearcuts, kinder clearcuts? Part of the problem is that a lot of us don't actually know what we want, so that's the first step. I know what I want. I want to live in a world that has more wild salmon every year than the year before. And I want to live in a world that has more migratory songbirds every year than the year before. And I want to live in a world that has less dioxin in every mother's breastmilk every year than the year before. So, first having figured out what

I want, then the next step is to figure out, how do we get from point A to point B? Once again, this is something that we often forget.

One of the things that everybody has said today is that we need to fight back. We need defiance, and we need organized resistance. So Aric, the first question is, what if we *don't* get that?

Aric McBay: Let's get the doom and gloom out of the way. It's critical that we have no false hopes, and that we have no illusions about the situation we're in.

Near the end of our book *Deep Green Resistance*, we lay out four different scenarios for the future of the planet, based on whether or not people fight back effectively. In the first scenario, there is no effective ecological resistance. It's just business as usual.

So, we start with peak oil. Conventional oil production has already peaked, and the effects will really take hold between about 2011 and 2015, resulting in a rapid decline in global energy availability. Some economists believe the recent economic downturn is just the first sign of peak oil. In any case, once peak oil truly sets in, the increasing cost and decreasing supply of energy will stall industrial manufacturing and transportation globally. This means that the markets will undergo economic turmoil and a self-perpetuating cycle of economic contraction.

And that part is the good news in this scenario. The bad news is that those in power will try to maintain their status by whatever means they can. With energy supplies in permanent decline, that means that they will intensify their exploitation of those on the bottom, especially for manufacturing, resource extraction, and agriculture. It will probably mean a resurrection or an intensification of institutions that many people think are basically defeated. Feudalism. Fascism. Slavery. Remember that two hundred years ago, before petroleum, 75 percent of the human population was in some form of serfdom or slavery. That's the nature of civilizations. After petroleum has been exhausted, those in power will try to return to the same arrangement. Without organized resistance, they'll be largely successful.

Of course, there will be a turn toward alternative energy, like solar panels and biofuels. But solar or wind power will not provide enough energy to run industrial society as it stands, and there won't be enough energy left anyway to build that alternative infrastructure on a global scale. The finite supply of concentrated energy in petroleum will have already been squandered on big cars, big televisions, and big wars. Coal will be used in large quantities, but it's not portable enough for most uses, and it emits even more carbon than petroleum.

As for biofuels, well, just because you have biofuels doesn't mean that you have a just and sustainable society. For example, the Nazis used a biofuel-powered V2 rocket to bombard England during World War II. The fuel was made from fermenting potatoes. The cotton plantations of the antebellum South were technically organic. That doesn't make slavery one iota less odious.

Now, the result of the decline in energy supplies will mean that agricultural production will be diverted into biofuels for the global rich. Without organized resistance to ensure that people's basic needs for food are prioritized over the demands of the rich, there will be mass hunger.

As industrial society crumbles, the effects of global warming will finally take hold, although the worst effects won't take place until decades after the oil is gone. There is a lag effect. The oceans, already emptied out by industrial fishing, will turn acidic and die. The Amazon rainforest, which currently produces its own climate by transpiring moisture, will turn into a desert, and other fragmented tropical forests will follow.

By then, there will be very little energy or industrial capacity left for humans to try to compensate for the effects of global warming. And as intense climate change takes over, ecological remediation through permaculture, perennial polycultures, and forest replanting will become impossible. The heat and drought will turn forests into net carbon emitters, as northern forests die from high temperatures, pests, and disease. Global warming will become self-sustaining and permanent.

Resource wars between nuclear states will break out. War between the U.S. and Russia is less likely than it was during the Cold War, but ascending superpowers like China will want their piece of the global resource pie. Nuclear powers such as India and Pakistan will be densely populated and ecologically precarious, as climate change will dry up major rivers previously fed by melting glaciers. With few resources to equip or field a mechanized army or air force, nuclear strikes will seem an increasingly effective action for desperate states.

Nuclear war or not, long-term prospects are dim. Global warming will continue to worsen long after fossil fuels are exhausted. The time to ecological recovery will be measured in tens of millions of years, if ever. As James Lovelock has pointed out, a major warming event could push the planet into a different equilibrium, one permanently hotter. It's possible that large plants and animals might only be able to survive near the poles. All that is required for this to occur is for current trends to continue without substantive and effective resistance. All that's required for evil to succeed is for good people to do nothing. The bottom line: Without real action to stop industrial civilization, we're doomed.

But this future is not inevitable. We have the basic tools and strategic ideas required to prevent this. What we need is organization, mobilization, and courage. The actual infrastructure that's destroying the planet has to be targeted, and the political and economic systems responsible must be dismantled.

Derrick: Okay, so what would that kind of action or strategy look like?

Aric: Well, for me, the key idea is a two-pronged strategy. In *Deep Green Resistance*, this is laid out in the fourth scenario. We try to imagine what a plausible and victorious struggle might look like.

There are two goals. The first is to disrupt and dismantle industrial civilization; and thereby to remove the ability of the rich to steal from the poor and the powerful to destroy the planet. And the second is to defend and rebuild just, sustainable communities, autonomous human communities; and as part of that, to assist in the recovery of the land.

These are two halves of a complete movement. Neither of them will work alone. We need to foster just and sustainable communities, because they're the only communities worth living in, and they are the only communities with a real future. We must help the natural world recover, because we need it to survive, and even more because the creatures of that world are our kin. Stopping industrial civilization is a prerequisite to achieving these things in the long term. We must stop it if there will be any real future.

On each half of this movement there is a whole spectrum of action. There is a place for everyone who wants to act. For those who choose to disrupt and dismantle civilization, resistance could look like tree sits or blockades. It could look like the shutting down of oil depots, as happened in France in 2010, or the shutting down of the port in Oakland in 2011. Or it could look like the direct attacks on infrastructure carried out by groups like MEND. For those who choose to rebuild and revitalize, resistance could look like growing food. It could look like rebuilding community. Or it could look like rebuilding cultures of resistance through protest and acts of defiance. Often, of course, these two sides overlap. Moreover, the two sides will proceed together, or they won't proceed at all.

There's an idea on the liberal Left that we can win simply by setting a good example. That won't work. Those in power didn't become powerful through some misunderstanding, but through conquest, exploitation, and genocide. No plan can succeed through attempting to persuade those in power. Any successful strategy will work through using some combination of political, economic, and physical force.

Successful strategies are also rarely based on abstractions. Few people will fight or take risks for abstract ideas. People will fight—and I don't just mean violence, but all kinds of fighting—for things that are real to them, like their families, their communities, the land, their culture. The more concrete and the more immediate the goals—or the more imminent the harm—the more likely people are to fight for them.

What we need is a long-term strategy that proceeds in stages, and each of those stages must have concrete and attainable goals. We must have a spectrum of action that can mobilize as many people as possible. We must have tactics that can actually help us achieve the goals with the people we have or the people we can get in the time available. Above all, the strategy must dramatically cut the burning of fossil fuels, and it must do so very soon.

We describe such a strategy in the penultimate chapter of *Deep Green Resistance*, in a chapter called "Decisive Ecological Warfare." In the book we look over many different potential plans and strategies to evaluate them strategically, but this is the overall trajectory.

Here is the scenario. A serious ecological resistance movement progresses through four different phases to bring about the two goals we talked about before: first, disrupting and dismantling industrial civilization, and second, defending and rebuilding just, sustainable communities. The movement includes both militant and moderate action, both aboveground and underground activists, and it encompasses a spectrum of tactics that range from low-risk community action like organizing and gardening to high-risk acts like mass sit-ins and sabotage. All of this happens globally. Let's talk about the four phases of this resistance movement.

Phase I: Networking and Mobilization

In the beginning of this scenario (as in the real world, now), resistance is mostly diffuse, and fragmented. The goal of the resisters in the first stage is to build up an organized resistance. In order to do this,

- They have to bring together diffuse resistance organizations, helping them to extend and coalesce.
- They have to build a *culture* of resistance, with all that entails.
- They have to build aboveground and underground resistance networks, and ensure the survival of those networks.

Networking and mobilization is facilitated by ensuring that people understand how to build movements that can exercise political force by studying historical resistance movements. Low-risk actions such as holding movie nights and workshops and book clubs may help with this, but people have to relearn for themselves how to be effective, which will only be done through action.

Again, Phase I is about building networks, both aboveground and underground, that can resist political repression.

Phase II: Sabotage and Asymmetric Action

In the second phase, these networks begin to take more serious action. They begin to choose infrastructure targets to shut down based on good target selection criteria. This involves two steps:

- Resistance networks identify and engage individual high-priority targets. These targets may be chosen by the resisters because they are especially attainable, but hopefully they are also very critical and not very recuperable. In other words, resisters in this phase may go after especially egregious targets—coal-fired power plants or exploitative banks—but they should still stick to small targets that they know they can defeat to build momentum.

+ Resistance networks give training and real-world experience to cadres necessary to take on the bigger targets and systems.

Again, this all has to happen both underground and aboveground. Aboveground organizations can mobilize the large numbers of people needed for civil disobedience, blockades, and the like. The underground organizations, of course, will never have those numbers, but they can directly disable machinery again and again without getting caught.

Aboveground and underground groups are often most effective when they work together on a campaign. The work of Canadian militant group Direct Action is a good example of this. In one case, there was a struggle in the 1980s to stop Litton Industries, near Toronto, from manufacturing components for cruise missiles. The direct aboveground protests were flagging, so Direct Action blew up a part of the plant. It didn't entirely go as planned—you can read about it in Ann Hansen's memoir, *Direct Action: Memoirs of an Urban Guerrilla*—but the action revitalized the aboveground movement, and huge protests and civil disobedience followed. Because of this combination of aboveground and underground action, the U.S. government pulled the manufacturing contract.

Other Phase II goals include exposing weak points in the system, demonstrating the feasibility of material resistance, and inspiring other resisters. That's very important, because without a culture of resistance, most people think that it's impossible. It's important for resistance networks to establish the rationale for taking action and to establish and grow parallel institutions. People need practice, they need to build their organizations, and they need to show people that it is actually possible to resist.

Phase III: Systems Disruption

In the next phase, resistance networks start to reach a critical mass. They are experienced enough to go after entire systems. So they might decide to shut down a specific corporation, like the group "Stop Huntingdon's Animal Cruelty" aimed to do.

In terms of runaway global warming, the major problems are fossil fuel industries, so resistance networks decide to shut down entire distribution systems for oil, coal, or gas. This means, again, aboveground and underground organizations taking action and looking for bottlenecks. So they wouldn't just try to shut down one coal-burning plant. They would shut down an entire coal-carrying rail network. Aboveground groups might do that with physical blockades. Underground groups might sabotage rail lines. Both are careful to target infrastructure in a way that avoids harming humans.

The point of this stage is to accelerate the industrial collapse that will already be underway. It works in concert with the fact that oil is already in shorter and shorter supply, and that the capitalist economy, a pyramid scheme, is in deep trouble.

It's at this stage that things like local food and the transition town movement really start to get popular. Most people will be interested in the convenience that comes from industrial capitalism as long as it is functioning smoothly—as long as it's still exploiting the poor and the planet effectively. Only when it starts to break down do real alternatives become possible.

While those on the front lines are shutting down the infrastructure that's killing the planet, there is another, much larger group of people working to rebuild local, democratic political structures. They are growing local food. They are rebuilding sustainable communities with all that entails. They are building the strong social movements and organizations that will be able to thrive after industrial capitalism is gone.

Phase IV: Decisive Dismantling of Infrastructure

In the last phase, resisters continue to escalate. They don't just disrupt systems or impair their functioning. They actually start to dismantle the infrastructure that's destroying the planet—mountaintop removal, coalmines, fracking rigs, dams, everything.

The main reason I am describing this is to try to get people thinking in a concrete and serious way about what kind of strategy will actually save the planet. This is not some kind of edict, and even the best strategic ideas are not easy to translate; they don't directly translate into the real world.

Moreover, I'm sure that some people will balk at the language of "decisive ecological warfare" and accuse us of being warmongers or something like that. But I know of no other word that expresses the life-and-death situation that we're in, the daily violence carried out by industrial civilization. Pretending that we're at peace won't help us, any more than it would have helped the people of Czechoslovakia, or Poland, or Russia in World War II.

It's not our fault that we're in this situation, and I don't think anyone here wanted this. But it's our responsibility to deal with it. The dominant culture is already at war with Indigenous people, and the poorest of the planet, with the land itself. And it wages this war daily.

It's important to remember that almost every raw resource this culture uses—from petroleum to metal ores to agricultural land—has been taken by force from traditional and Indigenous cultures. That's not just historical. That's current, that's right now. If you could shut down every site where raw materials are being pillaged from Indigenous land, the industrial economy would grind to a screeching halt tomorrow.

Derrick: You're talking about destroying infrastructure, but the thing we hear all the time is that if you burn it down, they're just going to rebuild. So what's the point?

Aric: They may or may not rebuild or repair an individual target, but the reality is that economic disruption is extremely effective. I'll give you some examples.

We know that the environmental movement has been largely unsuccessful at stopping, or even slowing, the destruction of the planet. So let's compare that to the effects of the major economic downturn that began in 2008, which had many beneficial effects for the planet. Electricity consumption dropped by several percent, which is the first time that global electricity use has declined since World War II. And this decline was because of a reduction in heavy manufacturing. If that electricity were from coal-fired plants, which of course much electricity is, then that decrease in electricity consumption would save so much coal that you could shut down half of all coal mining in India.

In Michigan, at the same time, twenty counties decided to de-pave their roads because it was too expensive to maintain them. Landfills across the United States reported a 30 percent decline in incoming garbage. Amazon rainforest deforestation was down almost 50 percent in 2009. It was the best year for the Amazon rainforest since they started keeping records. And I believe that a coordinated resistance movement can do an even better job than a random economic glitch.

In any case, of course some people will always say that there's no point in resistance, and that those in power will just rebuild. So our job, and the job of any serious resistance movement, is to turn that on its head, to make those in power say, "Well, there's no use in rebuilding it—they'll just shut it down again."

Derrick: Could you discuss Sobibor?

Aric: Sure. Sobibor was a concentration camp in Poland in World War II. Almost half a million people were killed there during the time that it operated. Eventually people decided that it was time to organize a resistance, and as they were trying to do this, a group of Russian Jewish POWs were brought in. They hatched a secret plan where they would have a spontaneous uprising with a small group of trained, prepared people. The resisters found a way to get Nazi officers separated off in one place, and they killed them—almost all of them, simultaneously. Something like six hundred people broke out of the camp, and many of them ended up surviving until the end of the war. Hitler was so embarrassed that he had the whole camp shut down, dismantled, and replanted with forest.

They don't always rebuild. And this is yet another example of how the people who fought back have a higher survival rate than the people who don't.

Derrick: So for resistance groups today, what's going to stop everybody from just getting arrested?

Aric: Well, we have very powerful tools and practices that we can use to protect ourselves and our movements from arrest and disruption. And we do need to be able to protect ourselves. We know that since the 1960s, operations like the FBI's Counter-Intelligence Program, COINTELPRO, have deliberately infiltrated and disrupted all kinds of leftist political groups, from social justice organizations to groups like the Black Panthers. COINTELPRO successfully destroyed many of them.

Now, we need multiple layers of protection. The first layer of protection is activist security culture. That means there are certain things that you should generally not ask other people about, like whether they are part of an underground group, or whether they've participated in illegal actions. Don't talk about illegal actions in a place where you might be bugged. Everyone should read "Security Culture: A Handbook for Activists," which is short, straightforward, and available online. You can also read a summary of another talk I gave about security culture, and watch the video, at deepgreenresistance.org.

Part of security culture is refusing to talk to police about activist groups or activities when they come around asking questions. So here's another piece of recommended viewing: "Don't Talk to Cops," which is a two-part video online (viewable on youtube.com) in which a lawyer and a police officer both argue that you should never answer police questions. This is not just for activists, this is for everybody. They are very convincing.

It's important to understand that these rules are not just for "illegal" or underground groups. Any effective program will be targeted—the FBI was just as afraid of the Black Panther meal programs as they were of armed militants. But the bottom line is that by following certain basic rules, we can increase our safety and decrease our paranoia. It's all based on need to know, and once you understand the basics, it becomes common sense.

The second layer of protection is a division between aboveground and underground. Aboveground and underground groups are fundamentally different kinds of organizations with fundamentally different rules.

We all know aboveground groups, which are organizations that work transparently and publicly. In contrast, underground groups work secretly and follow very tight security rules. So aboveground groups maximize their effectiveness through the use of wide communications and networking; they mobilize large numbers. Underground groups maximize their effectiveness by working secretly, by taking on work that can only be done in a clandestine fashion.

So why do people work underground? Well, the word will make many of us think, of course, of groups like the Weather Underground, the Animal Liberation Front, or the Earth Liberation Front. But people through history have formed underground groups for many different reasons. The Underground Railroad. Escape lines for persecuted people in Nazi-occupied Europe. Samizdat, the dissident literature network in the Soviet Union. Underground groups have a long, honorable, and extremely important history in the broader struggle for social justice.

Now, underground organizations have different rules that we may not be familiar with. The most fundamental rule is the firewall between aboveground and underground activity. That means that no one should be active in both underground and aboveground political organizations.

Let's take an example. When the French Resistance first formed after Germany invaded, resisters created all kinds of different groups with different rules and different structures. But they soon coalesced into two basic kinds of organizations: movements and networks. So movements had large numbers, they were relatively easy to join, and they were based mostly around underground newspapers. Networks were small, more selective, and organized around a specific objective like gathering intelligence or sabotaging rail lines. These are roughly analogous to aboveground and underground groups. So the French developed a rule that you couldn't belong in a movement and a network at the same time, because it put everyone at risk. That's the essential tenet of a firewall.

A second organizational rule, related to the first, is compartmentalization. An underground organization is made up of compartmentalized affinity groups or cells. People in a given group know people in their immediate group, but they don't know many people in the rest of the organization. That means if an affinity group is infiltrated, or if someone in that group is captured and tortured or turns, then the problem is contained to that cell, it doesn't take down the whole organization.

As an example, the African National Congress in apartheid South Africa had a rule that you were only allowed to know ten other people in the underground organization. And in stronger security states, stronger surveillance states, that number has been lower.

Also as part of their general security practice, underground groups are very careful about who they recruit and how. They have all kinds of screening practices, and many of them are discussed in the chapter on recruitment in *Deep Green Resistance*.

Now, the idea of people being arrested is obviously not a hypothetical one for radical environmentalists. Many people have been arrested in the Green Scare. The largest group of people were arrested in what the FBI called "Operation Backfire." Dozens of people were accused of dozens of different underground environmental actions.

They made mistakes. They didn't use compartmentalization, and they had too many people for a single cell. They didn't follow some of these basic rules, I think in part, because they thought of themselves as working informally, and not as a part of a proper organization.

Most people involved in "Operation Backfire" are now in jail because one member—Jake Ferguson, a heroin addict—became an informer for the FBI after the fact. He went around with a wire and talked to people, some of whom had been long "retired," and he got them to reminisce about the good old days. This reveals that the network had some breaches of security culture and proper screening, since Jake should probably never have been part of the group. In general, the arrests in the Green Scare, in this group and more generally, have *not* been a result of forensics or any fancy CSI crime scene investigation. They have all been because an informer or infiltrator talked to police when they shouldn't have.

Almost every new resistance movement starts with a wave of people who are arrested or killed. And the success of that movement is determined by whether that movement can a) support those casualties and then their families, and b) learn from those mistakes and move on.

We can all use the best security culture in the world, and we can learn from every mistake of the past, and some people are still going to end up in jail as soon as any movement starts to actually be effective, as soon as that movement starts to threaten the entitlement of those in power. Any resistance involves risk. So the question is: do we want to be as safe as possible, in the short term anyway, or do we want to be as effective as possible?

In *What We Leave Behind*, another work that you and I wrote together, Derrick, we said, "The question of how those in power respond to different actions is certainly strategically valid. But in a culture of resistance, it's not a reason to not resist by whatever means are most appropriate and effective. Of course those in power will try to inflict reprisals on those who resist them. Of course they will try to frighten and terrorize dissidents into accepting their authority. Of course they will try to harm even those who do not directly participate in actions against power. That's not a reason to hold back—*that is why we fight them*."

As we also said in that book, the dominant culture, the enemy, is already committing genocide. They're already skinning the planet alive. If we make them really mad, what are they going to do, destroy the planet twice?

Derrick: The question about what's going to stop everyone from getting arrested reminds me of one of my favorite lines from a resister ever. It was spoken by Zoya Kosmodemyanskaya. I don't know if I'll be able to say this without crying. She was a Russian partisan in World War II, and was caught by the Germans and tortured and mutilated. She didn't give up any information except her name, and she gave them the wrong name. And when they went to execute her, to murder her, the next day, the last thing she said was, "You can't hang all two hundred million of us." There's power in that. No matter how repressive they are, they can't kill all of us.

Having said that, they can sure try. Having said that, it's really scary to fight back. We hear a lot about lifeboats. Frankly, with the system collapsing, wouldn't it be better to just sort of batten down the hatches, protect you and your family, and hope that the storm doesn't actually kill you?

Aric: Well, the problem with just heading to the lifeboats is that this is not a *temporary* crisis or conflict. If we fail to stop this culture, then much of the planet may be uninhabitable for many thousands of years. And if we want to stop runaway global warming, we need to see decisive action in the next decade or so. If we don't act, there will be nothing left.

I'm not saying this to criticize people who are doing work like building local food systems and working with local energy—transition-type things. I'm an organic farmer, and I do plenty of these things myself. It's necessary, but it's not sufficient. Because if we can't stop the destruction of the biosphere and the climate, then all of that work will be wiped out.

If that isn't enough to convince you that lifeboats aren't sufficient, consider this: a little more than five centuries ago, this continent was filled with tens of thousands of sustainable, and often very democratic, Indigenous communities. Any five-year-old child among them was better at identifying wild edible plants than I will ever be. This continent abounded with warriors who were skilled and courageous beyond my conception. And yet they were all but wiped out by the insane civilized using tools and weapons that are hopelessly crude by modern standards. Do civilized people, many of whom are essentially novices both to living in healthy communities and living sustainably, think that they can survive so much better than Indigenous nations with countless millennia of uninterrupted experience?

And, of course, some people say, "Well, they'll see how great the Indigenous way of life is and they'll be converted." But do you really think that such communities will be perceived as a good example by those in power? I mean, look to history, look what happened whenever an empire met Indigenous people. Here is what Christopher Columbus wrote when he first encountered the Indigenous peoples of the Caribbean, his impression: "They are very gentle without knowing what evil is, without killing, without stealing." What did he conclude from this? "They will make excellent servants."

The dominant culture is voracious, and it's insane. All of these things emphasize the importance of a two-pronged approach of building up communities on one hand, and building up the land and defending them on the other.

I understand that not everyone wants to be on the front lines. But it's important to remember that only a small percentage of any resistance movement is actually on the front lines of the conflict. Not everyone has to risk their freedom or their lives to save the planet. But we all have to give support to front-line resisters, be it moral or material. (That includes writing to prisoners, for example.) It's fine and good for people to focus on growing food or healing people if that's where their skill or passion is. But, for both moral and strategic reasons, I think that we each have to take on the most radical action we can. Because right now we're still very outnumbered, and still sorely lacking in militancy.

A few minutes ago I talked about the Indigenous peoples of this continent during the European invasion. Though they won many battles though bravery, skill, and their knowledge of the land, it was extremely difficult—and is extremely difficult—to win prolonged military conflicts while an empire is still expanding. In fact, it's almost impossible to win as long as an empire still has a large supply of raw resources to consume.

But now we have some advantages they didn't have at the time, including examples of resistance over the past several centuries from which we can learn. And those empires are on the decline now; they are coming to the end of their supply of raw resources, and we can accelerate that process. The concentration of industrial infrastructure makes those empires vulnerable in a way they weren't only a few hundred years ago. There are opportunities here for decisive resistance. But if we just bury our heads in the sand, then we give up those few slim advantages we do have now.

Derrick: Going back to the example of resistance during World War II, there were many plots, of course, to attempt to kill Hitler and stop the Nazi atrocities. When the Allies invaded France, many of the plotters thought that they should just call it off, because the war was basically over they didn't want to take the risk. They thought, the Nazis are going to lose, so let's just take care of ourselves. But Henning Von Tresckow said, "No, the Nazis are killing twelve thousand people every day. So every day sooner that we can bring down the Nazi regime saves twelve thousand innocent lives." So even though it seemed inevitable that the Nazis were going to lose, they still proceeded and risked their own lives, and many of these people were tortured and killed because they wanted to stop those twelve thousand innocent murders every day. Now, two hundred species are being driven extinct every day. And every day sooner that we can stop it is a day sooner that we can save two hundred species.

Having said that, a lot of people understand that the industrial economy is really bad. But what about the fact that disrupting it could mean hunger, bands of looters, that sort of thing? And frankly, isn't resisting civilization the same as committing genocide?

Aric: Well, first of all, there will be no instantaneous collapse. Rome wasn't built in a day, and it didn't fall in one either. Collapse will proceed in stages. How we intervene won't change that—it will only affect how those stages play out and what's left when it's all over.

That said, let's start with hunger. How much oil does farming actually use right now, and will cutting oil use impact that? The reality, of course, is that the vast majority of oil used in North America goes to industry and the military. In fact, in the United States, the agricultural sector accounts for less than 2 percent of all energy use, including both direct consumption (like tractor fuel) and indirect consumption (like synthetic fertilizers and pesticides)—2 percent! That's true even though industrial agriculture is incredibly inefficient and uses something like ten calories of fossil fuel energy for every calorie of food energy it produces. And right now, half of all food is simply wasted. So you could reduce energy consumption dramatically without affecting that small amount of energy that's being spent on agriculture right now.

Of course, the benefit of living in a society that's incredibly wasteful is that you can trim a lot of excess before you start to get down to the actual necessities. And even then, there are, of course, fundamental changes that need to be made in the things, in the way that we get food and shelter.

Derrick: So if you cut back on energy use, maybe you're not going to kill a lot of people, but you're going to make it so you can't have retractable stadium roofs. Did you ever think about that?

Aric: I think about that every day. That's why I do this.

Here's another example for discussion: In Haiti, more than 99 percent of the trees have been cut down, currently mostly to make charcoal, because people have very limited supplies of other energy. They use it for fuel. People talk about that fact, but they rarely talk about the decades-long U.S. military dictatorship of Haiti in the beginning of the twentieth century, when Haiti was forced to export resources to pay debt. Think about this for a moment: you could supply one-quarter of all the energy Haiti uses with the gasoline Americans spill every year filling their lawnmowers. Hunger or deprivation is almost never about an actual shortage of supplies. It is almost always about inequality and exploitation.

Now, it's understandable to be concerned about how the disruption of industrial society will affect people living here, but the effects of a properly functioning industrial society are ghastly around the world. Look at the destruction of the Niger Delta. Or think about the fact that in the Democratic Republic of Congo, millions of people have been killed, and millions more women raped, in a war fueled by the looting and export of minerals like coltan. Coltan is an ore used to make capacitors for computers and cell phones. So we're the ones paying for that war.

Or think about the fact that there are parts of India where half of all hand-dug wells are now dry. Industrial drilling based on oil technology has drawn down the water table so much that people just can't dig deep enough to get it. Every day this culture continues, it closes off more options for long-term subsistence and survival.

There is also a compelling argument to be made that the disruption of the industrial economy in the privileged world is vital to help people prepare for its inevitable and eventual collapse. Dmitry Orlov, who's an expert on the collapse of the Soviet Union, wrote, "After collapse, you regret not having an unreliable retail segment, with shortages and long bread lines, because then people would have been forced to learn to shift for themselves instead of standing around waiting for someone to come and feed them." So, by the time Soviet Union actually collapsed, plenty of people were already growing their own food out of necessity. So they were better able to cope.

Even if you don't think we should stop burning all oil, think about what that last big gush of oil is being spent on. Big-screen TVs and international tourism for the globally rich (which is most of us, by the way). Pointless wars. The construction of buildings and suburbs that won't even be inhabitable after the oil is gone. And it will be gone very fast in historical terms. So isn't it better to try to reduce oil production and transport now, with a simultaneous movement for social justice? That way, if the oil supply is disrupted, there will be a push to spend what remains on actual necessities instead of luxuries for the globally rich. That would extend the period in which at least a little oil is available to cope. Of course, I'm just talking about humans. I think it's clear that the daily existence of industrial society is bad news for just about every nonhuman species on the planet.

Look, we know what the endpoint of this culture is. Industrial collapse won't be easy, but it's better than a global ecological collapse. This culture is coming down anyway. If we engage with the process of collapse, we can guide it in a less destructive direction, rather than letting those in power have control.

For me the ultimate question isn't whether people will be hungry if there is some hiccup in global capitalism. The question is, how do we stop the hunger and deprivation this culture is already causing, and the far worse deprivation and conflict it will create as it tries to continue in the face of all ecological limitations?

As for looters, frankly, I'm not as worried about hypothetical looters twenty years in the future as I am about the team of professional looters running the government and the economy.

Derrick: When things get really bad for the planet, will there be a mass movement that will rise up in the United States to do something?

Aric: I don't think so. Part of the problem, of course, is that once global warming, and many other problems, get really bad for the privileged people of the world, it will be too late.

I study resistance movements, and so I've spent a lot of time studying resistance to the Nazi occupation in Europe. There was vigorous resistance in many countries, but very little within Germany itself. When I have asked people about that, some of them have told me it's because people were afraid of the SS and the Gestapo. But, of course, the SS and the Gestapo killed people in the occupied countries as well.

And then I came across a public opinion survey that was taken in Berlin in 1952. People were asked whether, had the crimes of the Nazis been known, resistance against the Nazis would have been justified. And keep in mind this survey was conducted after the Nuremberg trials; everyone knew about the concentration camps and the medical experiments. They weren't asked whether *they* would participate in resistance—because obviously, for almost all of them, the answer was "no"—they were only asked whether it was justifiable. Only 41 percent of them said "yes." When the question was modified to ask whether resistance would have been justifiable in wartime—which in any empire is constant—the number of people who said "yes" dropped by half.

The majority of people identified so strongly with those in power in Germany that they were unable to oppose the Nazis, even theoretically, even after the fact, and even after the Nazis had committed unimaginable crimes against humanity. Sometimes a revolution is a prerequisite to a mass movement. Sometimes changing consciousness takes too long—especially when the bulk of people are somehow benefitting from the status quo.

Perhaps the majority of Germans didn't agree with resistance, but what about people who actually saw the worst of it? What about average people who went to the concentration camps? Psychologist Bruno Bettelheim, a survivor of both Dachau and Buchenwald concentration camps, gives us the answer. He wrote, "*Non-political middle class* prisoners (a minority group in the concentration camps) were those least able to withstand the initial shock. They were utterly unable to understand what had happened to them and why. More than ever they clung to what had given them self-respect up to that moment. Even while being abused, they would assure the SS that they had never opposed Nazism. They could not understand why they, who had always obeyed the law without question, were being persecuted. Even now, though unjustly imprisoned, they dared not oppose their oppressors even in thought, though it would have given them a self-respect they were badly in need of." And he goes on to talk about how many of those nonpolitical, middle-class prisoners betrayed those who were trying to organize resistance in the camps to the SS in hopes that they would get some kind of favors.

So no, I don't think that we'll see a mass movement in time to save the planet, even if things get really bad. At least, not in the wealthier parts of the world. And I think that's very important for us to understand. Most people will not break their identification with the dominant culture in time. We can't afford to wait around for a mass movement that isn't coming. We have to use tactics that will be effective with the number of people we already have or that we can reasonably expect to get.

Derrick: Right now, it doesn't look like a lot of people in the United States or among the global elite are fighting back. What will it take?

Aric: Some people are fighting back, and they're mostly Indigenous people, poor people, and others who've been pushed to the margins, who have little left to lose. In this country, there is a new movement called Deep Green Resistance that hopes to carry out the above-ground work that we're talking about here, the aboveground of this movement. You can get more information at deepgreenresistance. org. These people are committed, and I think that anyone who cares about the future of the planet should think about joining up or supporting them.

No resistance movement starts fully formed. They develop over time, and sometimes they do so very slowly or they must overcome major setbacks. Take the Abolition movement prior to the Civil War in the United States. Early white opposition to slavery focused on "moral suasion." Abolitionists would actually visit slaveholders and try to convince them to free their slaves. They would argue that slavery was immoral, or that it was an affront to God, and they actually convinced some people. Of course, their success was limited, especially in the South.

At the same time, the Underground Railroad continued to grow and develop. There's a misapprehension that the Underground Railroad was mostly run by well-meaning white people. But, of course, it was run mostly by black people, like Harriet Tubman. In a good year, the Underground Railroad might rescue hundreds or even thousands of people. The problem was that despite this, the population of enslaved people continued to grow through birth.

Some people decided that success would only come by attacking the institution of slavery directly. And one of those people was John Brown. Brown would go to Abolitionist meetings and then complain afterward about how much people talked. He said, "What we need is action! Action."

Brown created a plan, and it was a plan that many historians believed could have worked very well, if it weren't for some obstacles he came up against. His plan was to take a group of fighters to seize the government armory at Harper's Ferry, in Virginia (now West Virginia). They would seize the armory and the weapons it contained, and then they would disappear into the South. From the hills and the backwoods they would wage a kind of defensive guerrilla warfare, moving from plantation to plantation, and liberating the slaves, some of whom would join the fight. Soon, the plantations would be emptied out, and the slave economy would collapse.

It was a good plan, but obstacles arose from the very beginning. Brown had hoped to have a thousand fighters to start with. On the day of the raid, only twenty showed up. But Brown decided they had to do what they could with who they had, and they went ahead with the raid. They did capture the armory, but instead of maintaining the mobility that guerrillas need, they stayed there. When some of the townspeople tried to recapture the armory, they took those people prisoner and let them order out for breakfast and visit their families under escort. This delay gave the army enough time to march over from the next town. So they defeated John Brown's fighters, most of whom were hanged.

Most white people didn't support Brown. Even a lot of Abolitionists were opposed to what he tried to do. But Brown had been trying to avoid violence. He saw the writing on the wall. He knew that the growth of slave power meant that a bloody civil war was inevitable if slavery wasn't stopped.

And, of course, he was right. Within a year of him being hanged, civil war did break out. And it was the bloodiest single war in

American history, with more American soldiers killed than in all
other wars, before or since, combined. Even many Abolitionists had
failed to understand what a fundamentally violent system slavery
was, and thought that it could be resolved without using force. But
they were wrong. And millions of people died because of it.

I think there are clear parallels to our own situation. We want to
be nice. We want to avoid conflict, and maybe avoid causing trouble.
But if we fail to stop this culture, the results for humans and for the
planet will be far more violent than the conflicts we are trying to
avoid.

I'll end with some thoughts on the French Resistance. When
France was invaded in 1940, people were deeply shocked and disori-
ented. A few years earlier it had been hard to imagine that the Nazis
could so quickly conquer Europe, so resistance developed slowly.
Early ideas of resistance privileged spiritual resistance, and even
fashion. Underground newspapers published articles about how the
"elegance of Parisian women" constituted a form of resistance; they
looked just so damn elegant, won't that spite the Nazis?

Around 1943, the situation changed suddenly. There was a dra-
matic rise in the number of resistance sabotage actions and assas-
sinations. Underground newspapers that had been writing about
spiritual resistance started printing editorials saying that it was the
duty of every French person to assassinate Nazi officers and para-
militaries. So what changed? The difference was that by 1943, it
started to look as though the Nazis might *lose the war*. When the
Nazis stopped looking invincible, people started to fight back.

Again, the parallels to our own situation are clear. With peak oil,
food crises, economic collapse, and so on, the cracks in the façade are
starting to show. Industrial capitalism is not invincible. It is not going to last forever. As in France, it's time for a shift to a more serious
organized resistance. And I think we can win.

Arundhati Roy

"We don't talk about justice anymore. None of us do; we just talk about human rights or survival. We don't talk about redistribution. In America, four hundred people own the wealth of more than half of the American population. We should not be saying *tax the rich*, but instead we should be saying *take their money and redistribute it, take their property and redistribute it.*"

Derrick Jensen: Arundhati Roy is a world-renowned author, public intellectual, and political activist best known for her novel *The God of Small Things*, and for her uncompromising work for environmental and social justice.

Arundhati Roy: There are so many things that I want to say, but let me start by saying that every kind of resistance that has been discussed here in theory is being carried out in practice where I live. To begin with, I want to salute the people who live in one of the poorest countries in the world—India—for stopping some of the biggest corporations in their tracks for the last five or six years. Let's just say, "Salaam."

I don't know how far back in history to begin, so I'll lay the milestone down in the recent past. I'll start in the early 1990s, when capitalism won its war against Soviet Communism in the bleak mountains of Afghanistan. What I'm going to talk about is roughly what happened in the last twenty or so years. The Indian government, which was for many years one of the leaders of the nonaligned movement, suddenly became a completely aligned country and began to call itself the natural ally of the U.S. and Israel. It opened up its protected markets to global capital. Most people have been speaking about environmental battles, but in the real world it's quite hard to separate environmental battles from everything else: the war on terror, for example; the depleted uranium; the missiles; the fact that it was the military-industrial complex that actually pulled the U.S. out of the Great Depression, and since then the economies of places like America, many countries in Europe, and certainly Israel, have depended largely on the manufacture of weapons. What good are weapons if they aren't going to be used in wars? Weapons are absolutely essential; it's not just for oil or natural resources, but for the military-industrial complex itself to keep going that we need weapons.

Today, as we speak, the U.S., and perhaps China and India, are involved in a battle for control of the resources of Africa. Tens of thousands of U.S. troops, as well as death squads, are being sent into Africa. The "Yes We Can" president has expanded the war from Afghanistan into Pakistan. There are drone attacks killing children every day there.

Let's discuss the process of how things panned out in India. In the 1990s, when the markets of India opened, when all of the laws that protected labor were dismantled, when natural resources were privatized, when that whole process was set into motion, the Indian government opened two locks: one was the lock of the markets; the other was the lock of an old fourteenth-century mosque, which was a disputed site between Hindus and Muslims. The Hindus believed that it was the birthplace of Ram, and the Muslims, of course, use it as a mosque. By opening that lock, India set into motion a kind of conflict between the majority community and the minority community, a way of constantly dividing people. Finding ways to divide people is the main practice of anybody that is in power.

The opening of these two locks unleashed two kinds of totalitarianism in India: one was economic totalitarianism, and the other was Hindu fundamentalism. These processes manufactured what the government calls "terrorism." You had Islamist terrorists and you had what today the government calls "Maoists," which means anybody who is resisting the project of civilization, of progress, of development; anybody who is resisting the take-over of their lands or the destruction of rivers and forests, is today a Maoist. Maoists are the most militant end of a bandwidth of resistance movements, with Gandhists at the other end of the spectrum. The kind of strategy people adopt to resist the onslaught of global capital, is quite often not an ideological choice, but a tactical choice dependent on the landscape in which those battles are being fought.

Nearly everybody is considered a Maoist. Just this morning I received an e-mail from India about an Indigenous tribal woman who was just arrested a few days before I left India. She's now being held and tortured and asked to name some of us as the "overground leaders of the Maoist movement," which is absolutely ridiculous.

Since 1947, ever since India became a sovereign republic, it has deployed its army against what it calls its own people. Now, gradually, those states where the troops were deployed are states of people who are fighting for self-determination. They are states that the decolonized Indian state immediately colonized. Now, those troops are actually defending the government's rights to build big dams, to build power projects, to carry out the processes of privatization. In the last fifty years, more than thirty million people have been displaced by big dams alone in India. Of course, most of those are Indigenous people or people who live off the land.

The result of twenty years of this kind of free market, and this bogey of terrorism, is in the hollowing out of democracy. I notice a lot of people using the word *democracy* as a good word, but actually, if you think of it, democracy today is not what democracy used to be. There was a time when the American government was toppling democracies in Latin America and all over the place. Today, it's waging wars to install democracy. It has taken democracy into the workshop and hollowed it out.

In India, every institution, whether it's the courts, or the parliament, or the press—has been hollowed out and harnessed to the free market. There are empty rituals to mask what actually happens, which is that India continues to militarize, it continues to become a police state. In the last twenty years, after we embraced the free market, 250,000 farmers have committed suicide, because they have been driven into debt. This has never happened in human history before. Yet, obviously when the establishment has a choice between suicide farmers and suicide bombers, you know which ones they are going to encourage. They don't mind that statistic, because it helps them; they feel sorry, they make a few noises, but they keep doing what they are doing.

Today, India has more people than all the poorest countries of Africa put together. It has 80 percent of its population living on less than twenty rupees a day, which is less than fifty cents a day. That is the atmosphere in which the resistance movements are operating. Of course, it has a media—I don't know any other country with so many news channels, all of them sponsored or directly owned by corporations, including mining corporations and infrastructure corporations. More than 99 percent of all news is funded by corporate advertising, so you can imagine what's going on with that. The prime minister of the world's largest democracy, Manmohan Singh, who was more or less installed by the IMF, has never won an election in his life. He stood for one election and lost, but after that he was just placed there. He's the person who, when he was finance minister, actually dismantled all the laws and allowed global capital into India.

One time I was at a meeting of iron ore workers, and Manmohan Singh, the prime minister of that time, was the leader of the opposition in Parliament. A Hindi poet read out a poem called "What is Manmohan Singh doing these days?" The first lines were: "What is Manmohan Singh doing these days? What does poison do after it enters the bloodstream?" They knew that whatever he had to do was done, and now it's just a question of it taking its course.

In 2005, which was the second term of the present government, the Indian government signed hundreds of Memorandums of Understanding, or MOUs, with mining companies, infrastructure companies, and so on, to develop a huge swath of forestland in Central India. India has one hundred million Indigenous people, and if you look at a map of India, the minerals, the forests, and the

Indigenous people are all stacked up, one on top of the other. These Memorandums of Understanding were signed in with these mining companies in 2005. At the time, in the state of Chhattisgarh, which is where this great civil war is unfolding now, the government raised a tribal militia, which was funded by these corporations, to basically go through the forest to try and clear it of people so that the MOUs could be actualized. The media started to call this whole swath of forest the "Maoist Corridor." Some of us used to call it the "MOUist Corridor." Around that time, they announced a war called "Operation Green Hunt." Two hundred thousand paramilitary began to move into the forests, along with the tribal militia, to clear it of what the government called Maoists.

The Maoist movement, in various avatars, has existed in India since 1967, which was the first time there was an uprising. It took place in a village in West Bengal called Naxalbari, so the Maoists are sometimes called Naxalites. Of course it's an underground, banned party. It now has a People's Liberation Guerrilla Army. Thousands of people have been killed in this conflict. Today, there are thousands of people in prison, and all of them are called Maoists, though not all of them are *really* Maoists, because as I said, anybody who resists today is called a terrorist. Poverty and terrorism have been conflated. In the Northeastern states we have laws like the Armed Forces Special Powers Act, which allows soldiers to kill on suspicion. In all of India we have the Unlawful Activities Prevention Act, which basically makes even thinking an antigovernment thought a criminal offense, for which you can be jailed for more than seven years.

This is the atmosphere that was being created, and the media was in this orgy of these "Maoist-terrorists." They were conflating them with the Lashkar-e-Taiba, so you'd see them on TV with ski masks and AK-47s, and the middle class was literally baying for their blood. At this time, I had written a couple of articles about the whole thing, television anchors would look around at me like I was crazy when I mentioned mining. What was the connection between pure evil guerrillas and good mining corporations? In my book, *Field Notes on Democracy*, there's a part about how the Supreme Court of India actually gave a judgment saying you cannot possibly accuse a corporation of malpractice. In so many words, it just says so.

Derrick: One of the sentences that you said you have heard a lot is *we'll give away our lives, but never our land.* Can you talk about that?

Arundhati: More than ten years ago, I wrote about perhaps the biggest nonviolent, Gandhian, anti-dam movement, the Narmada Bachao Andolan. As I said, dams alone have displaced more than thirty million people, and with today's neoliberal economic policies, the biggest issue that is causing unrest across the country is displacement and the take-over of people's lands. In the Narmada movement, people would stand in their homes while the river rose to protest in that way, but it just didn't matter, and the dams kept going up. Today, they are building about one hundred dams in the Himalayas in Arunachal Pradesh, which is a very thinly populated area.

When mining companies want to take over your land, you can defend your land if you're organized. But if it's a question of a dam, it's harder. The biggest dam of the Narmada project, the Sardar Sarovar Dam, is being built in Gujarat, which is a completely fascist state, but the submergence, the reservoir, is in the other states. It's not as though *people* are coming to take over your land; the thing you love the most, your river, is rising to take over the land. You can't shoot the river; you can't blow up the river. How do you fight a dam? You can fight it if you prevent it from being built in the first place, but if it's being built, the site can be secured militarily, as are the sites in the Northeast.

If you look at the history of the struggle for land in India, what is really sad is that after India became independent, land reform was one of the biggest things on the agenda of the new government. This was of course subverted by the politicians, who were upper-class people, landowners. They put so many caveats in the legal system that absolutely no redistribution happened. Then, in the 1970s, when the Naxalite movement started, when the first people rose up, it was about the redistribution of land. The movement was saying *land to the tiller.* It was crushed; the army was called out. The Indian government, which calls itself democratic, never hesitates to call out the army. Today, people have completely forgotten the idea of redistribution. Now, they are fighting just to hold on to what little they have. We call that "progress." The home minister says he wants 70 percent of India to live in cities, meaning he wants five to six hundred million people to move. How do you make that happen, unless you become a military state? How do you do that, unless you build big dams and big thermal projects and have nuclear power?

In so many ways, we have regressed. Even the most radical politics are practiced by people that are privileged enough to have land. There are millions and millions of people who don't have land, who now just live as pools of underpaid wage labor on the edges of these huge megalopolises that make up India now. The politics of land in one way is radical, but in another way it has left out the poorest people, because they are out of the equation. We don't talk about justice anymore. None of us do; we just talk about human rights or survival. We don't talk about redistribution. In America, four hundred people own the wealth of more than half of the American population. We should not be saying *tax the rich,* but instead we should be saying *take their money and redistribute it, take their property and redistribute it.*

Derrick: I love this line you wrote: "Justice—that grand, beautiful idea—has been whittled down to mean human rights."

Arundhati: I actually hate that phrase, "human rights." What does it mean? I want justice. That's what I was getting at, in that we can't just isolate the environmental battles. At the keystone of the arch has to be the idea of justice, because all of these things eventually do coincide. In India, I would still say that environmentalists, as a group, are pretty reviled by people's movements, because they are elitist; they are the ones who want the national parks emptied so that you can save the tiger; they don't understand the meaning of justice at all. In fact, these wars—like the one that I'm talking about—are ones in which people are also part of the ecosystem.

As someone who stands on this side of the line, who stands with this bandwidth of resistance movements, I do turn around and ask the comrades some questions, such as: "Will you leave the bauxite in the mountain?" Today, one of the biggest battles being fought in India is over the extraction of bauxite, the ore that makes aluminum, which is at the center of the military-industrial complex. There's something like four trillion dollars' worth of bauxite in the mountains of Orissa and Chhattisgarh. Bauxite mountains are beautiful; they are flat-top mountains. Bauxite is a porous rock, and when it rains the mountains absorb the water; they are like water-tanks. They let the water out through their toes, and they irrigate the plains. Mining companies, who have bought the bauxite for a small royalty to the Indian government, have already traded it on the future's market. For local people, the bauxite in the mountain is the source of their life and their future, their religion and everything. For the aluminum company, the mountain is just a cheap storage facility. They've already sold it, so the bauxite has to come out, either peacefully or violently.

Now, the Indian government—the largest democracy in the world—is planning to call out the army in Central India, to fight the poorest people in the world.

Derrick: You have written, "Gandhian *satyagraha* is a kind of political theater. In order for it to be effective, it needs a sympathetic audience, which villagers deep in the forest don't have. When a posse of eight hundred policemen lay a cordon around a forest village at night and begin to burn houses and shoot people, will a hunger strike help? Can starving people go on a hunger strike? And, do hunger strikes work when they're not on TV?"

Arundhati: We were talking earlier about different strategies of resistance, and these are life debates in India; not just among the government, or academics, but between resistance movements, too. There is very real tension, because sometimes an armed guerrilla action can be extremely irresponsible. It can do something that invites repression from the state, or even from the fascist Hindu militias also operating on behalf of the state. A lot of the Indian government's violence and repression is outsourced to the mob; it's not always acting as a state. Often, academics or journalists or these moronic anchors in TV studios will initiate a debate based on the question, *is violence moral or immoral?* (SMS your answer to the studio now.)

Of course, people don't necessarily function like that. You can be a Maoist in the forest and a Gandhian on the street. You can change identities based on what suits you tactically; it's not like you have to swear to be this thing or that thing or the other thing. Some people do, some don't. I think what happens in India is that there is something false about this debate, because it's infused with a kind of false morality. After all, if people from the middle class were to support that fight—which is an oxymoron; they won't—then I can understand you saying we should all get together and go on a hunger strike. But, if you're going to distance yourself from that village that has been surrounded by a hundred policemen and is being burned, then it's immoral to try and lecture to those people how they should protect themselves.

Derrick: A lot of what we're talking about, and a lot of what I write about, scares me. I'm wondering if you get scared.

Arundhati: Often, people describe me as brave. It gives me a rash, because I think it's really important to be scared. It's really important to know what you're up against. And, it's really important to not have a martyr complex; it's important not to want to go to jail and not to want to die, and yet, to do what you have to do to be effective, and to know what you're good at doing. I grew up in a small village in South India. When I recently spent time in the forest with the comrades, it was lovely to be in the forest and to have only whatever it was I carried on my back. I asked them, "Shall I just stay here?" They said, "No." Because you've got to do what you've got to do, and you've got to do what you're effective at doing. I think of it as a kind of waltz; you've got to know when to step forward and when to step back, and when to wait and when to move—and, to enjoy it.

Quite often, when you see what is being done to people, it creates rage in you and humiliation if you keep quiet. People ask me why I write, and I say it's in order to not be humiliated. I don't write for anything else except to not be humiliated. Every time I write, I keep telling myself that I won't do it again, but it's like I can't contain it inside my body; I write, and it's a relief.

To answer your question, I think it's important to be scared. I won't say that I'm not scared, but I suspect that I'm more scared of keeping quiet, because as a writer, if you know something and then you keep quiet, it's like dying. Between the various choices of fear, I still choose to write rather than not write.

For many years, I have been writing and following resistance movements and the new economic policy. I've always found that the chances of coming upon despair are much greater in middle-class households, than on the ground where people are actually fighting. Middle-class people have the choice between hope and despair, just like they have the choice between shampoo for dry hair and oily hair; they have the choice between doing politics and interior design. People who are fighting don't have a choice; they are fighting and they are focused and they know what they are doing. They are arguing with each other a lot, of course, but that's all right.

When I landed in New York, one of the first things I did was to go to the Wall Street occupation, because I wanted to see who they were, what it was about, and how it connected to the things that we've been fighting and writing about. Regardless of what all of the various trends are, and the fact that the movement doesn't have demands, and that it doesn't have identifiable leaders, there is clearly still a connection between what is going on in the Occupy movement and what is going on in India. That connection is that of exclusion. These are people who are excluded. They are clearly not the four hundred families who own half of the wealth of America. They are not the hundred people in India who own 25 percent of India's GDP.

While many of us believe in revolution, and believe that the system must be brought down, right now, the least we can ask for to begin with is a cap on all of this. I'm a *cappist* and a *liddite*. We do need to say a few things: one is that no individual can have an unlimited amount of wealth. No corporation can have an unlimited amount of wealth. This sort of cross-ownership of businesses really has to stop.

In India, the Tatas are the biggest company. They own iron ore mines, steel mines, iodized salt, and television channels. They manufacture trucks, they fund activists, they do everything. There's an iron ore and steel company called Gindels. They have iron ore mines, steel mines. The CEO is a member of Parliament. He's also a member of National Flag Foundation, because he won the right to fly the national flag on his house. They run a global law school just outside Delhi, which is like a Stanford campus in the midst of the most unbelievable squalor you can imagine. They have faculty flown in from all over the world paid huge salaries. They fund and promote cutting-edge artists who work in stainless steel. They recently had a protest workshop where they flew in activists to this unbelievably posh campus and then had protest poetry and protest slogans. They own everything; they own the resistance, the mines, the Parliament, the flag, the newspapers. They don't let anything go. These are some simple things that have to stop. Berlusconi owns 90 percent of the media in Italy; so what if he's not the prime minister?

It's a kind of insanity that could have some simple solutions, too. For example, perhaps children shouldn't inherit the wealth their parents amass. We can all find some simple solutions like this that would point us in the right directions.

Q&A with Arundhati Roy and Derrick Jensen

Question: Derrick, you mention in some of your books that if we're honest with ourselves, hunting and gathering is the only sustainable level of technology. I was wondering if the world you envision post revolution is at that hunter-gatherer level, or if you see some kind of hybrid that is possible.

Derrick: It seems pretty clear to me that any way of life that is based on the use of nonrenewable resources is by definition not sustainable. Likewise, any way of life that is based on the hyperexploitation of renewable resources is not sustainable. If every year there are fewer salmon than the year before, eventually there will be none.

I would then go a step further and say that any way of life that is based on the use of resources won't last. What I mean by that is that so many Indigenous people have said to me that the fundamental difference between Western and Indigenous ways of being is that even the most open-minded Westerners conceive of listening to the natural world as a metaphor. They conceive of the natural world as resources to be exploited instead of other beings to enter into relationships with.

This is really crucial because how you perceive the world affects how you behave in the world. There's a great line by a Canadian lumberman: "When I look at trees I see dollar bills." If when I look at trees I see dollar bills, I'm going to treat them one way. If when I look at trees I see trees, I'm going to treat them another way. If when I look at this particular tree I see this particular tree, I treat it differently still.

The same is true for fish, the same is true for bauxite mountains, the same is true for women. If when I look at women all I see are orifices, I'm going to treat them one way. If when I look at women I see them as women, I'll treat them another way. If when I look at this particular woman I see this particular woman, I'll treat her differently still.

I just saw a great example of this. I live in a coastal town, and in the newspaper the harbor master was explaining why crabbers work so hard during the crabbing season: "Each crab is worth about a dollar fifty, and if you can imagine a bunch of envelopes lying all over the ground and each one has a dollar fifty in it, you'd be picking them up as fast as you can." And that's true, except crabs aren't actually envelopes filled with a dollar fifty; crabs are beings with lives as valuable to them as yours is to you and mine is to me. Which doesn't mean that we can't eat them.

I was on a radio show in Spokane, Washington, and the interviewer said "You know, Indians exploited salmon too." And I said, "No they didn't, they ate them." And he asked, "What's the difference?" And I said, "They gave them respect of the spirit in exchange for the flesh."

I knew that answer was kind of crap, but I'm a male and thus required by law to answer every question anyone asks of me. Later on I had a conversation with a tree I had a long relationship with, where I asked, "What is the fundamental predator/prey relationship?" The tree gave me the answer right away, which is, "If you consume the flesh of another, you take responsibility for the continuation of the other's community."

So if I take salmon from the Klamath River, I take responsibility for the continuation of the Klamath River salmon community. Not stewardship, which comes from the root *sty ward*, which means the ward of the pig sty; but instead "responsibility," which comes from the root *respondere*, which means "to give in return." So they give me their life, and I give them mine.

But back to the original point. No, the only level of technology that is sustainable is that which does not harm the landbase at all. Eventually, by definition, we will all be living that way or we won't be living at all.

Where I live is Tolowa land, and the Tolowa lived there for 12,500 years, if you believe the myths of science. If you believe the myths of the Tolowa they've lived there since the beginning of time. That's a long, long time. The dominant culture has been there 150 years and the place is trashed. We can fantasize all we want, but the only level of technology that is sustainable is one that is not based on the exploitation of nonrenewable resources or the hyperexploitation of renewable resources.

Question: There has been wide criticism of the Occupy movement based on the privilege of those who are a part of it and the lack of narrative of communities of color and low-income folks. What is your advice on bridging multiple and diverse struggles?

Arundhati: I think that it's interesting that it's the reverse of what happens in a place like India, where the privileged people are not involved in movements unless they are very right-wing movements. Even the antiwar movement. I remember being here to participate in a march and being interested in the fact that there were not that many black people or other people of color involved. Even in this audience, there aren't that many people of color. I'm not exactly the right person to answer that question, but I think perhaps it does have to do with the fact that they don't even have the leisure time to be involved.

I don't know if I'm right about that, but for example, when you're trying to mobilize politically in a city, the people who are really at the bottom of the barrel have to work so hard night and day to eat that they don't have time to be involved. They simply can't afford to. The old days of labor unions have been dismantled. Derrick, do you have a better answer?

Derrick: No. But being a male, I'll give an answer anyway, which is that there is a term for what you're talking about. It's called "primary emergency," which means that if someone has the time to become an activist, a lot of times they will work on the primary thing that is affecting them. Many times, when a woman becomes an activist, one of her first issues may be violence against women. I think primary emergencies are central to how people choose issues to work on.

Question: I notice you're using bottled water. When we look at technology, are we making the decision that some of it is okay?

Arundhati: I think that the appearance of bottled water is a terrible thing, and it's quite recent. I come from the state of Kerala, the southern-most part of India, where there is a huge, quite successful agitation against Coca-Cola, because obviously they have the money to get the biggest drills and they are pulling out the water for bottled water. All the farms nearby are drying up because Coca-Cola is pulling out all the water. Just like cities will not enhance public transport, which means people have to drive cars, they won't clean up the water system for the sake of providing clean drinking water, so everyone has to buy water in plastic bottles.

A few years ago, there was a world water conference at the Hague, and I had just written this big piece on dams so they asked me to go. I wasn't going to initially, but then I read that the Indian government was sending an entire delegation to ask for funds to build more dams. So I just kind of arrived to wreck the proceedings as much as I could. I was put on this panel that was supposed to be a panel of writers, but I was the only writer actually on it. The others were writers of policies. In the lobby of that meeting were all these people dressed up as faucets. The whole meeting was to press for the privatization of water. Each of us had to introduce ourselves and say why it was that we wrote about water. There was a man next to me from America who said, "I write about water because I'm paid to." Then he said, "I just want to say that god gave us the rivers but he didn't put in the delivery systems, and for this we need private enterprise."

I was up next and I said, "I'm Arundhati Roy and I write about water because I'd be paid a great deal not to." The conference was such a display of wanting to own everything, just everything, and sell it, then resell it to us. Fundamentally, people like that want to own language, which I suppose is my primary emergency issue as a writer.

I remember at that meeting saying, "I've never been in a room full of dead people for such a long time." Because as a writer, you spend your life trying to minimize the distance between language and thought. You try to describe exactly what you're thinking, exactly what you're feeling. And here I was, in a room full of people doing exactly the opposite, devising a language with which to mask thought. They used words to mean the opposite of what they really mean. To even retrieve our language is a battle.

Derrick: I want to go at this from a slightly different direction. Lierre Keith said, "The task of an activist is not to navigate systems of oppressive authority with as much personal integrity as possible, it is to take down those systems of oppressive authority."

I remember talking with an Indigenous friend of mine, Jeanette Armstrong, who is an Okanagan activist and writer, and I said, "Oh, my god, I feel so bad because I drive a car and global warming is all my fault." She said, "Take responsibility for what you do. You didn't invent car culture, and your job is not to minimize your own personal actions within it, your job is to take down car culture."

In an essay I wrote a few years ago titled "Forget Shorter Showers," I talked about how we always hear that the world is running out of water and the cure is to take shorter showers, and so on. But that displaces responsibility onto individuals instead of the whole system. More than 90 percent of all water is used by agriculture and industry, so if you take a shorter shower, all that will really do is ruin your social life. Municipal golf courses use as much water as municipal people. So that's where the real action lies.

It's the same with trash. I'm not saying that one should not try to minimize consumption as much as one possibly can, but that's not where action really is. The average person in the U.S. produces about 2,600 pounds of trash per year. So let's say I reduce that to zero. I don't buy anything with any packaging whatsoever, I wear my tennis shoes until they fall off my feet, I repair my toaster, and so on. That's great, but the problem is that the average per capita production of trash in the U.S. is about 2,600 pounds. Of that, 97 percent is agriculture and industry, again. So we can reduce our personal production to zero, but that's not where the real action is.

This is what pisses me off so much about movies on environmental issues. They lay out all the problems, but in the end all the solutions are personal. They don't talk about the larger issues. *Food Inc.* really made me angry. The whole movie is great, discussing how the agricultural system is concentrated, it's unsustainable, and it's exploitative. But one of the solutions is to buy yogurt from Walmart. There's this disconnect at the end. I think that there is altogether too much concern with personal purity in the environmental movement and in the Left in general.

Arundhati: I think you should try living as an activist in the land of Gandhi, where unless you wear a loincloth and don't have sex and eat goat cheese, you're a bad person. That whole idea of "you have to be a saint first and then be political" is also a way of making sure that a whole lot of people are not political.

Question: I'm an organizer for Occupy San Francisco, and a lot of people, especially those occupying twenty-four/seven, are displaced people. My question is, doesn't this bring the picture closer to home?

These are people who are setting up camps and feeding each other, providing medical care, and they're being violently attacked by the state. Do you think that this will lead to more militant action, more acts of property destruction?

Arundhati: First of all, you must tell the people who are doing that that the fact that this is happening in America is an inspiration to the rest of the world. I'm sure that it's the other way around too, because it's extremely important for the information to go both ways. I would also say that it's unlikely that the state will tolerate the occupation of territory for too long. It will hit a point where they feel threatened, and they will not tolerate that.

Some kind of a system that allows you to dispose and regroup in ways where the police won't know where you will be next, or how or when, will be necessary. It will have to turn into a sort of guerrilla occupation where you don't hold territory. Because you can't hold territory against the most powerful military in the world, unless it's in the forest or something. The state will jack up its level of violence when it feels threatened. So the politics will have to evolve to a different space other than just trying to hold territory.

Question: How can the resistance continue when it is dependent on the very system it is taking down for food and for organization?

Derrick: I think Aric addresses this when he talks about the fact that only 2 percent of the oil is used in the U.S. for agriculture. Look at World War II and the conversion of the economy to a war economy. There are a lot of things that can be done before it is the global elite starting to feel the brunt of deficiency. That's part of it.

Also, if the global economic and transportation system is interdicted enough that the resisters can no longer communicate or move around, I think that means we've won. At that point I think it would be reduced to local fights.

Question: What should you do to make colleges the moral centers of communities that they are supposed to be, instead of producers of evil scientists, elites, and workers?

Arundhati: The system of colleges here is different than India, although India is getting there. Increasingly, corporations are funding colleges, then setting the agenda for the education. Obviously, that needs to stop. You can't have corporations deciding on the pedagogy in a college. In places like India organizations like the Ford Foundation have sort of a benign self-image, and they fund a lot of causes, but they slowly train people to be creatures of the free market. They fund people who do certain things, and withhold funding when people choose something else. So people choose what gets them funded.

The conflict of interest is so huge that, once again, it's almost humiliating to be put into that system, and, for most people, to not even know it. Obviously, colleges have to return to being publicly funded institutions. Of course, we're not even talking about student loans and the fact that you have to take huge loans to get this corporate education, then not get a job but still have to repay the loan.

Derrick: There's a reason that when the democracies of Central and South America were destroyed by U.S. and corporate interests, one of the places they'd hit first were universities. One of the great things that a university can provide is a mix of people who have the leisure to theorize with people who have directly felt the iron boot of oppression on their necks. That can be an absolutely incendiary combination of theory and reality.

Those in power have recognized that, so places like Central and South America have a kind of colonial model for their universities, with cops going in to repress the students. In the U.S. we have privatization and the free market going in; those in power are saying, we're not going to shoot you, but we're going to pay you to do what we want you to do.

Arundhati: In India, education has become one of the biggest rackets. As the government pulls back on public funding, these fly-by-night institutions of business management have emerged. They're attended by families who have just about entered the middle class, because of this whole free market thing; they live in rough neighborhoods, and they are so terrified of their children turning "bad" that they pay a lot of money to these institutions, where they get basically nothing in return. The families go into debt, but these institutions vacuum up millions. Quite a frightening scenario.

Question: What can you say about the role of Indian-Americans in supporting Indigenous Indian struggles in India?

Arundhati: First of all, I must clarify the fact that Indigenous resistance is not the only resistance happening. There is all kinds of resistance, and the neoliberal privatization is not only affecting Indigenous people. The fact is that a majority of Indian-Americans, particularly the Information Technology population in places like Silicon Valley, and many who come to study and work in the U.S., generally are very much part of an elite class. A lot of them do act politically, but they generally support the right wing. When I write, and I get letters saying, "She should be hanged," a lot of them are from people who are part of this elite. This is something I'm sure a lot of you could work to counter.

There was a time at the beginning of the World Social Forum that I did think that international solidarity was something we should put a lot of time into. But then I realized that a lot of the best activists just turned into travel agents. I would say that it's also not necessary to think in terms of "I'm an Indian-American, what can I do for India?" What you can do in the place that you live is just as important.

Sometimes, I don't even know what people mean when people talk about India. I think the most successful secessionist movement has been the secession of the middle and upper classes into space, where they sort of look down at the people and say, "What's our bauxite doing in their mountains?" and, "What's our water doing in their rivers?" They have colluded with the elite in the rest of the world. The Indian elite considers itself part of America in some ways. India was one of the few countries where George Bush was very popular among the elite.

So I don't even tend to think in those ways anymore. I think we should just do what we can where we are.

Question: A lot of us here know we need to resist, but a lot of us don't know how; we're scared, we're trying to find a way to plug in. And it makes me think about that story you tell, Derrick, about the Warsaw Ghetto.

Derrick: Zygmunt Bauman writes about how the Nazis made it so that every step of the way it was in the Jews' best interest to not resist. When I talk about that, I usually end with something very important, which is that the Jews who participated in the Warsaw Ghetto uprising had a higher rate of survival than those who went along.

The Jews who participated in the Warsaw Ghetto uprising had a higher rate of survival than those who went along.

No, listen: the Jews who participated in the Warsaw Ghetto uprising had a higher rate of survival than those who went along.

Keep that in mind over the next ten years.

About the Participants

William Catton Jr. is a sociologist known for his work in environmental sociology and human ecology. He is the author of *Overshoot: The Ecological Basis of Revolutionary Change*. His most recent book is *Bottleneck: Humanity's Impending Impasse*.

Jane Caputi is a professor of American studies at the University of New Mexico. She is the author of *The Age of Sex Crime*; *Gossips, Gorgons and Crones: The Fates of the Earth*; and *Goddesses and Monsters: Women, Myth, Power, and Popular Culture*.

Riki Ott is a marine toxicologist, author, and former commercial fisher. She is the author of *Sound Truth and Corporate Myth$: The Legacy of the Exxon Valdez Oil Spill* and *Not One Drop: Promises, Betrayal, and Courage in the Wake of the Exxon Valdez Oil Spill*.

Nora Barrows-Friedman is a freelance journalist currently based in the West Bank and California. She was a senior producer for one of Pacifica Radio's flagship shows, *Flashpoints*.

Gail Dines is a professor of sociology and women's studies at Wheelock College in Boston, an internationally acclaimed speaker and author, and a feminist activist. She is the author of *Pornland: How Porn Has Hijacked Our Sexuality*.

Thomas Linzey is a public interest attorney and the executive director of the Community Environmental Legal Defense Fund, a nonprofit law firm that has provided free legal services to over five hundred local governments and nonprofits since 1995. He is also a cofounder of the Daniel Pennock Democracy School. Linzey is the author of *Be the Change: How to Get What You Want in Your Community*.

Waziyatawin is a Dakota writer, teacher, and activist committed to the development of liberation strategies that will support the recovery of Indigenous ways of being, the reclamation of Indigenous homelands, and the eradication of colonial institutions. She is most recently the author of *What Does Justice Look Like? The Struggle for Liberation in Dakota Homeland*.

Lierre Keith is a writer, radical feminist, food activist, and environmentalist. Her book *The Vegetarian Myth: Food, Justice, and Sustainability* has been called "the most important ecological book of this generation." Her most recent work is *Deep Green Resistance: Strategy to Save the Planet*, with Aric McBay and Derrick Jensen.

Stephanie McMillan is an award-winning cartoonist, the creator of the daily comic strip "Minimum Security." Her most recent book is *The Beginning of the American Fall: A Comics Journalist Inside the Occupy Wall Street Movement*. She has also coauthored several books with Derrick Jensen, including *As the World Burns: 50 Simple Things You Can Do to Stay in Denial* and *The Knitting Circle Rapist Annihilation Squad*. She is an organizer for One Struggle, an anticapitalist/anti-imperialist collective.

Aric McBay is an activist and small-scale farmer. He is the author of *Deep Green Resistance: Strategy to Save the Planet*, with Lierre Keith and Derrick Jensen, and *What We Leave Behind*, with Derrick Jensen.

Arundhati Roy is an Indian novelist and activist. She won the Booker Prize in 1997 for her first novel, *The God of Small Things*. Her most recent work is *Walking with the Comrades*.

Derrick Jensen is an award-winning activist, philosopher, and writer. Derrick is one of the most important voices of the environmental movement. His books include *A Language Older than Words*; *The Culture of Make Believe*; and *Endgame, Volumes I and II*.

About
PM Press

politics • culture • art • fiction • music • film

PM Press was founded at the end of 2007 by a small collection of folks with decades of publishing, media, and organizing experience. PM Press co-conspirators have published and distributed hundreds of books, pamphlets, CDs, and DVDs. Members of PM have founded enduring book fairs, spearheaded victorious tenant organizing campaigns, and worked closely with bookstores, academic conferences, and even rock bands to deliver political and challenging ideas to all walks of life. We're old enough to know what we're doing and young enough to know what's at stake.

We seek to create radical and stimulating fiction and nonfiction books, pamphlets, t-shirts, visual and audio materials to entertain, educate, and inspire you. We aim to distribute these through every available channel with every available technology, whether that means you are seeing anarchist classics at our bookfair stalls; reading our latest vegan cookbook at the café; downloading geeky fiction e-books; or digging new music and timely videos from our website.

Contact us for direct ordering and questions about all PM Press releases, as well as manuscript submissions, review copy requests, foreign rights sales, author interviews, to book an author for an event, and to have PM Press attend your bookfair:

PM Press • PO Box 23912 • Oakland, CA 94623

510-658-3906 • info@pmpress.org

Buy books and stay on top of what we are doing at:

www.pmpress.org

MONTHLY SUBSCRIPTION PROGRAM

These are indisputably momentous times—the financial system is melting down globally and the Empire is stumbling. Now more than ever there is a vital need for radical ideas.

In the four years since its founding—and on a mere shoestring—PM Press has risen to the formidable challenge of publishing and distributing knowledge and entertainment for the struggles ahead. With over 200 releases to date, we have published an impressive and stimulating array of literature, art, music, politics, and culture. Using every available medium, we've succeeded in connecting those hungry for ideas and information to those putting them into practice.

Friends of PM allows you to directly help impact, amplify, and revitalize the discourse and actions of radical writers, filmmakers, and artists. It provides us with a stable foundation from which we can build upon our early successes and provides a much-needed subsidy for the materials that can't necessarily pay their own way. You can help make that happen—and receive every new title automatically delivered to your door once a month—by joining as a Friend of PM Press. And, we'll throw in a free T-Shirt when you sign up.

Here are your options:

- $25 a month: Get all books and pamphlets plus 50% discount on all webstore purchases

- $40 a month: Get all PM Press releases (including CDs and DVDs) plus 50% discount on all webstore purchases

- $100 a month: Superstar—Everything plus PM merchandise, free downloads, and 50% discount on all webstore purchases

For those who can't afford $25 or more a month, we're introducing Sustainer Rates at $15, $10 and $5. Sustainers get a free PM Press t-shirt and a 50% discount on all purchases from our website.

Your Visa or Mastercard will be billed once a month, until you tell us to stop. Or until our efforts succeed in bringing the revolution around. Or the financial meltdown of Capital makes plastic redundant. Whichever comes first.

END:CIV

Resist or Die

Directed and Produced by Franklin Lopez
$20.00 • DVD • 75 minutes

END:CIV examines our culture's addiction to systematic violence and environmental exploitation, and probes the resulting epidemic of poisoned landscapes and shell-shocked nations. Based in part on *Endgame*, the best-selling book by Derrick Jensen, *END:CIV* asks: "If your homeland was invaded by aliens who cut down the forests, poisoned the water and air, and contaminated the food supply, would you resist?"

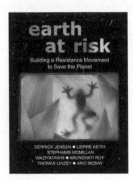

Earth at Risk

Building a Resistance Movement to Save the Planet

Edited by Derrick Jensen and Lierre Keith
$20.00 • DVD • 7 hours

The seven people in this film present an impassioned critique of the dominant culture from every angle One by one, they build an unassailable case that we need to deprive the rich of their ability to steal from the poor and the powerful of their ability to destroy the planet. These speakers offer their ideas on what can be done to build a real resistance movement, one that includes all levels of direct action—action that can actually match the scale of the problem.

Now This War Has Two Sides

Derrick Jensen
$19.99 • CD • 115 minutes

Examining the premises of *Endgame* as well as core elements of the *Culture of Make Believe*, this lecture and discussion offers both an introduction for newcomers and additional insight for those familiar with Derrick Jensen's work. Whether exposing the ravages of industrial civilization, relaying humorous anecdotes from his life, or bravely presenting a few of the endless forms that resistance can (and must) take, Jensen leaves his audience both engaged and enraged.

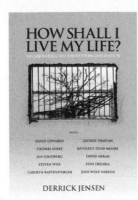

How Shall I Live My Life?

On Liberating the Earth From Civilization

Derrick Jensen
$20.00 • Paperback • 304 pages

In this collection, Derrick Jensen discusses the destructive dominant culture with ten people who have devoted their lives to undermining it.

Whether it is Carolyn Raffensperger and her radical approach to public health, or Thomas Berry on perceiving the sacred; be it Kathleen Dean Moore reminding us that our bodies are made of mountains, rivers, and sunlight; or Vine Deloria asserting that our dreams tell us more about the world than science ever can, the activists and philosophers interviewed in *How Shall I Live My Life?* each bravely present a few of the endless forms that resistance can and must take.

Other interviewees include: George Draffan, Jesse Wolf Hardin, David Abram, Steven Wise, Jan Lundberg, and David Edwards.

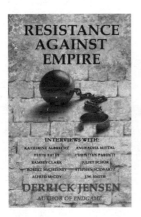

Resistance Against Empire

Derrick Jensen
$20.00 • Paperback • 280 pages

A scathing indictment of U.S. domestic and foreign policy, this collection gathers incendiary insights from 10 of today's most experienced and knowledgeable activists. Whether it's Ramsey Clark describing the long history of military invasion, Alfred McCoy detailing the relationship between CIA activities and the increase in the global heroin trade, Stephen Schwartz reporting the obscene costs of nuclear armaments, or Katherine Albrecht tracing the horrors of the modern surveillance state, this investigation of global governance is sure to inform, engage, and incite readers.

Other interviewees include: Robert McChesney, J.W. Smith, Juliet Schor, Christian Parenti, Kevin Bales, and Anuradha Mittal.

Truths Among Us

Conversations on Building a New Culture

Derrick Jensen
$20.00 • Paperback • 264 pages

This prescient, thought-provoking collection features ten leading writers, philosophers, teachers, and activists. Among those who share their wisdom here is acclaimed sociologist Stanley Aronowitz, who shows us that science is but one lens through which we can discover knowledge. Luis Rodriguez, poet and peacemaker, asks us to embrace gang members as people instead of stereotypes, while the brilliant Judith Herman helps us gain a deeper understanding of the psychology of abusers in whatever form they may take. Paul Stamets reveals the power of fungi, whose intelligence, like that of so many nonhumans, is often ignored. And writer Richard Drinnon reminds us that our spiritual paths need not be narrowed by the limiting mythologies of Western civilization.

Other interviewees include: George Gerbner, John Keeble, Marc Ian Barasch, Martín Prechtel, and Jane Caputi.

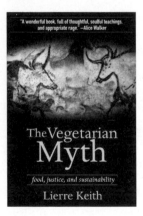

The Vegetarian Myth

Food, Justice, and Sustainability

Lierre Keith
$20.00 • Paperback • 320 pages

We've been told that a vegetarian diet can feed the hungry, honor the animals, and save the planet. Lierre Keith believed in that diet and spent twenty years as a vegan. But in *The Vegetarian Myth*, she argues that we've been led astray—not by our longings for a just and sustainable world, but by our ignorance.

The truth is that agriculture is a relentless assault against the planet, and more of the same won't save us. In service to annual grains, humans have devastated prairies and forests, driven countless species extinct, altered the climate, and destroyed the topsoil—the basis of life itself. Keith argues that if we are to save this planet, our food must be an act of profound and abiding repair: it must come from inside living communities, not be imposed across them.

Part memoir, part nutritional primer, and part political manifesto, *The Vegetarian Myth* will challenge everything you thought you knew about food politics.

Songs of the Dead

Derrick Jensen
$20.00 • Paperback • 320 pages

A serial killer stalks the streets of Spokane, acting out a misogynist script from the dark heart of this culture. Across town, a writer has spent his life tracking the reasons for the sadism of modern civilization. And through the grim nights, Nika, a trafficked woman, tries to survive the grinding violence of prostitution. Their lives, and the forces propelling them, are about to collide. This is a story lush with rage and tenderness on its way to being a weapon.

Lives Less Valuable

Derrick Jensen
$18.00 • Paperback • 208 pages

At the heart of a city, a river is dying, children have cancer, and people are burning with despair. From the safe distance that wealth buys, a corporation called Vexcorp counts these lives as another expense on a balance sheet. But that distance is about to collapse.

Three

Annemarie Monahan
$16.95 • Paperback • 320 pages

As a radical feminist, Antonia has never believed in band-aid political solutions. After years of planning, she and her lover found an independent nation for women on an abandoned oil rig.

Dr. Katherine North is not a sentimental woman. But after she reads that an old lover has died, she's driven to make peace with the woman who still haunts her.

Growing up working-class and Catholic, Kitty Trevelyan never considered abortion when she got pregnant at eighteen. Now, at forty-one, she no longer believes that life begins at conception, but knows that hers certainly ended with it.

Three very different women. All forty-one. With the same birthday. With the same birthmark. As the parallel lines of their lives converge, we realize what connects them: they were all once the same seventeen-year-old girl on an April morning, wondering whether she would be brave.

The Knitting Circle Rapist Annihilation Squad

Derrick Jensen and Stephanie McMillan
$14.95 • Paperback • 192 pages

The six women of the Knitting Circle meet every week to chat, eat cake, and make fabulous sweaters. Until the night they realize that they've all survived rape—and that not one of their assailants has suffered a single consequence. Enough is enough. The Knitting Circle becomes the Knitting Circle Rapist Annihilation Squad. They declare open season on rapists, with no licenses and no bag limits. With needles as their weapons, the revolution begins.

Will the Knitting Circle triumph? Or will Officer Flint learn to knit in time to infiltrate it? Will Nick the male ally brave Daisy's Craft Barn to secure more weapons for the women? Will Marilyn put down her teenage attitude and pick up her knitting needles? Will Circle member Jasmine find true love with MAWAR's (Men Against Women Against Rape) Zebediah?

Mischief in the Forest

A Yarn Yarn

Derrick Jensen • Illustrated by Stephanie McMillan
$14.95 • Hardcover • 40 pages

Grandma Johnson lives alone in the forest and loves to knit sweaters and mittens for her grandchildren in the city. One day, when returning from a visit to the city, her solitude comes to an end when her mischievous forest neighbors reveal themselves in a delightfully colorful fashion. Who took her yarn, and what have they done with it?

The colorful mystery is solved when the birds, rabbits, snakes, trees, and other dwellers of Grandma Johnson's neighborhood are seen playing with the yarn. Suddenly the forest doesn't seem so lonely, and the visiting grandkids take great delight getting to know the inhabitants of Grandma's forest. This picture book is a lesson for both young and old to connect with one's surroundings and embrace the role of good neighbors with the rest of the natural world, whether in the city or in the forest.